SQUALO

"In this compelling history of squa
construction, Renwick and Shilliam d
to cast today's squalid living conditions forced on many across
the UK as a matter of morality and show them to be one of
mortality. This is perhaps most poignantly exposed in their
discussion of the Grenfell Fire, a touchpoint throughout the book.
A truly significant contribution to the contemporary rethinking
of one of Beveridge's five impediments to social progress."

GURMINDER BHAMBRA, Professor of Postcolonial
and Decolonial Studies, University of Sussex

"A gripping read, *Squalor* powerfully describes
the long-term historical processes that have shaped
deprivation in our time. Left me feeling madly angry."

ARUN KUNDNANI, author of *The Muslims are Coming!
Islamophobia, Extremism, and the Domestic War on Terror*

"*Squalor* is a beautifully-written collaboration unified by the
authors' clear commitment to acknowledging, documenting and
detailing the organized and in many cases, purposeful negligence of
Britain's working classes. But its key achievement is its engagement
with a particular aspect of political education that focuses on the
evolution of regulations, which plainly demonstrate that housing,
or the right to a dignified life in one's home, should be the ultimate
unifier of the polity. This is a book which illuminates exactly why
everyone should be paying attention to the politics of housing."

CHANTELLE JESSICA LEWIS,
Pembroke College, University of Oxford

"This brilliant work treads the trajectory of spatial arrangement in
granular detail, and skillfully dispels several key myths along the journey.
It concretizes the macro decisions, taken at the highest levels of political
office, that have continually reordered the nitty-gritty micro level of
day-to-day life across the century. This is an indispensable resource in
the attritional war for the human right to safe and secure housing."

LOWKEY, hip hop artist and journalist

FIVE GIANTS: A NEW BEVERIDGE REPORT

Consultant editor: Danny Dorling, *University of Oxford*

In November 1942, William Beveridge published *Social Insurance and Allied Services*, the result of a survey work commissioned the year before by the wartime coalition government. In what soon became known as simply "The Beveridge Report", five impediments to social progress were identified: the giants of Want, Disease, Squalor, Ignorance and Idleness. Tackling these giants was to be at the heart of postwar reconstruction. The welfare state, including national insurance, child allowances and the National Health Service, was a direct result of Beveridge's recommendations.

To mark the eightieth anniversary of the Report's publication, the authors in this series consider the progress made against Beveridge's giants, and whether they have diminished or risen up to again stalk the land. They also reflect on how the fight against poverty, unfit housing, ill-health, unemployment and poor education could be renewed as the countries of the UK emerge from a series of deeply damaging, divisive and impoverishing crises.

As an establishment figure, a Liberal and a eugenicist, Beveridge was an unlikely coordinator of the radical changes that improved so many peoples' lives. However, the banking crisis at the end of the 1920s, the mass unemployment and impoverishment of the 1930s, and the economic shock of the Second World War changed what was possible to what became essential. Old certainties were swept aside as much from within the existing order as from outside it.

The books explore the topic without constraint and the results are informative, entertaining and concerning. They aim to ignite a broader debate about the future of our society and encourage the vision and aspiration that previous generations held for us.

Want by Helen Barnard

Disease by Frances Darlington-Pollock

Squalor by Daniel Renwick and Robbie Shilliam

Ignorance by Sally Tomlinson

Idleness by Katy Jones and Ashwin Kumar

SQUALOR

Daniel Renwick and Robbie Shilliam

agenda
publishing

First published in 2022 by Agenda Publishing

Agenda Publishing Limited
The Core
Bath Lane
Newcastle Helix
Newcastle upon Tyne
NE4 5TF

www.agendapub.com

ISBN 978-1-78821-388-2
ISBN 978-1-78821-389-9 (ePDF)
ISBN 978-1-78821-390-5 (ePUB)

British Library Cataloguing-in-Publication Data
A catalogue record for this book is available
from the British Library

Typeset in Nocturne by Patty Rennie

Printed and bound in the UK by CPI Group (UK) Ltd,
Croydon, CR0 4YY

Contents

Acknowledgements

This book could not have been written without the support of many individuals, authors and campaigns that we stood on the shoulders of in seeking our vantage points. We are forever grateful for the tireless activism of Grenfell United and the North Kensington community. Their fight for meaningful truth, justice and accountability is a constant source of motivation. Huge thanks also have to go to Kareem Dennis (Lowkey), Brenna Bhandar and Peter Apps who read and advised on early drafts of the book. The invaluable wisdom of Colin Prescod can also be traced, along with the legacy of the work of the Institute of Race Relations. Many thanks to Maryam Nahhal for editorial work. Thanks also to Alison Howson for invaluable editorial advice. Any mistakes or wrongful articulations are entirely ours.

Daniel Renwick
Robbie Shilliam

1

Introduction

Squalor simply defined: your habitat kills you. Squalor is inextricably bound to mortality and ever-increasing proximity to death caused by overcrowded quarters, damp abodes, polluted streets, and even petroleum-clad buildings. Some of these conditions are recognizably squalid and conjure conventional images of the poor and destitute. But some might surprise. For instance, consider the possibility that young professionals who stretch their budget to mortgage a leasehold in dangerously built apartment complexes are suffering from squalor. We know this giant from a hundred different books and films. We might not appreciate just how closely it stalks many of us.

Within squalor it is possible to find Beveridge's other giants gestating – want, disease, ignorance and idleness. Yet squalor is distinct in so far as it is the only giant that does not directly reference human faculties or needs. Squalor, instead, is a condition of the built environment in which humans live. Etymologically, squalor derives from the Latin *squalidus*, meaning, "to be covered with dirt". Squalor, then, intonates a covering over and defiling of humanity. The word has also come to imply a kind of osmosis between humans and their lived environment. Where the human ends and their habitat begins is unclear. For this reason, "good" homes and streets equals worthy humans, whereas "bad" homes and streets equals unworthy denizens.

The aim of this book is to provide a political history of squalor in Britain from the mid-nineteenth century to the present day. We are not interested in a past that is dead. Rather, we hope to provide a "history of the present", that is, a history that helps to illuminate contemporary challenges. Crucial questions that will guide this illumination include: what elements of squalor persist over time, and how are they part of the bedrock of British politics? How has squalor changed its form? What should we name as squalor in our present day? And, when it comes to slaying the giant of squalor, what are the forces of continuity and who are the agents of change?

The objective of this book is to demonstrate that squalor in Britain has been consistently re-made by political elites, even as they have pursued policies to ameliorate squalid conditions. This is not to claim that squalor is simply an intentional project. Rather, we argue that diverse strategies such as slum clearance, new town building, social housing provision, and buying incentives have all rested on a fatal flaw: those who live in squalor have been judged to be part of the dysgenic environment themselves – they are a part of squalor, rather than sufferers of squalid conditions.

Underpinning this judgement lies a moralizing discourse that blames the poor for not having the strength of character to replace the attitudes that reproduce squalor: licentiousness, recklessness and fecklessness. One logic of this discourse is to abandon and quarantine those denizens who, living in squalor, threaten to exert a dysgenic influence on society by spreading dependency, criminality and disorder. Another logic embraces a social uplift directed by patricians and targeted at humans who demonstrate they have the strength of character to extract themselves from a squalid fate.

Additionally, we argue that this moralizing pathology regularly racializes those living in squalor as less-than – or degeneratively – human. Even before postwar Commonwealth immigration, and even excepting Irish migrants, the poor in nineteenth-century

English cities were considered a "residuum" – a substance left behind, apart from the Anglo-Saxon race. This sense of being residual to society was oftentimes heightened with analogies to colonial subjects, even for residents of London's docklands. Of course, such racialization was far more direct and unforgiving when it was later targeted at South Asian, African Caribbean, African and Middle Eastern residents. That said, poor white families have continued to be subtly racialized as an underclass.

When it comes to squalor, race and class are co-implicated. This factor is consequential to our analysis. Re/de-valuing of populations along race/class lines has usually resulted in the building of new habitats to distance the deserving from the undeserving poor. At the same time the undeserving have been both dispossessed of their existing homes and placed in proxy habitats that, in fact, re-induce the same conditions of squalor. Connected to this fatal division are concrete policies such as land reclamation via gentrification, land valuation and speculation, wealth accumulation through rental markets, securitization of neighbourhoods, and the outsourcing and deregulation of local governance.

We track this process of population sorting across a historical vista constituted of imperial, welfare, neoliberal and populist eras. We demonstrate that the political elite of each new era reformulated the problem of squalor yet at the same time reintroduced conditions ripe for squalor. This is not to say that all elite projects are the same, even if they depend on similar logics. On the one hand, some projects sought to resist the impulse to segregate populations; on the other hand, some projects sought to replace a public duty to house almost entirely with a private interest to buy. In many ways, the consistent reproduction of squalor over time eventuates as much through the clash between various projects as the similarities of their premises and assumptions.

Besides elites, we also track a resistive project by those who have suffered squalor. The elite co-option of the word "community" is part of an attempt to categorize, sanction and direct potentially wayward peoples. Community is supposed to be resilient and breed independence, albeit at all times an orderly independence in the service of bureaucratic designs and private and corporate interests. But alongside this sense of community sits a "communalism". By this phrase, we refer to a bottom-up approach to shared space in predominately urban settings developed by the residents and denizens themselves rather than architects, planners, or state officials. Communalism evinces a distrust of the state and its services, and a desire for self-determination through methods sometimes considered illicit or even criminalized.

We believe that the reflex to pathologize criminality or deviance in communities, cultures or ethnicities must be recognized and interrogated. Actions that are considered deviant are oftentimes poverty-driven or at least derive from the requirements to survive in squalid living conditions. While the self-saboteur can live in a form of self-imposed squalor if they so wish, our ultimate concern is for the society that creates the consciousness that stews in misery or revels in crime. We do not seek to romanticize squalid conditions. For the purposes of this book, we make only a slim moral judgement on illicit modalities and their deleterious – or beneficial – effects on life chances. The environment that breeds the consciousness is our primary concern, and so we shall, on occasion, fold these counter-projects into the political story of squalor.

Above all, though, our story suggests that to slay the giant of squalor the moralizing division of good and bad residents must be done away with. To do so would implicate a profound rethinking of how we value land in a capitalist economy. As we shall conclude, such a rethinking is of direct relevance for an increasing number of people.

We begin, in Chapter 2, by revisiting the moral debates in Victorian Britain over squalor, with a special fixation on the poor inhabitants of urban centres. Philanthropists and pamphleteers worried that the poor might lose their health and characteristic self-reliance and instead become diseased, dependent and disorderly as they took root in the "dens" and "rookeries" of squalid inner-city areas. These people formed the "residuum" that pooled in the detritus of industry and trade. It is with regards to sanitizing the "residuum" that many of the foundational premises and propositions for ameliorating squalor were developed. We then examine how this moral discourse was integrated into a new science of urban geography provided by the likes of Charles Booth. Furthermore, we demonstrate that this science was given political salience when it was connected to the imperial standing of Britain in the aftermath of the South African War.

In Chapter 3, we turn from philanthropy to national planning in the lead up to – and aftermath of – the First World War. Inter-imperial competition combined with the influence of the Russian Revolution to produce a new era of housing policies exemplified by the premiership of David Lloyd George. In this era, government committed to undertake coherent social reforms for the sake of maintaining political order. Council house building and rent controls were used to ameliorate overcrowding and unsanitary conditions. Yet these policies tended to reproduce the distinction between the deserving and undeserving poor and so were unable to smooth the uneven nature of housing costs and conditions when it came to class and region. As a new world war began, it was clear that a more radical approach to housing was required – as with most welfare issues. The logic of Beveridge's report, however, failed to ameliorate the stark inequalities in housing provision and cost, especially when it came to his lauded universal principle of an "adequacy of provision". Beveridge's plan to slay the giant of squalor was, even by his own standard, unconvincing.

Chapter 4 turns to the post-Second World War context, otherwise known as the era of the "welfare state". We question the conventional wisdom that a consensus over welfare provision obtained between the two main parties. When it came to housing policies, Labour and the Tories held to quite different principles.

We lay out Nye Bevan's audacious plans to address squalor by creating mixed communities and establishing a principle of "general need" that would address the unevenness of housing provision and costs. We then track how the Conservative Party rolled back Bevan's policy innovations by replacing state-controlled provision of general needs with a state supported accommodation of private interests especially in terms of land value. We finish, however, by noting that a political consensus did exist when it came to the treatment of non-white Commonwealth residents who had settled in British towns. We suggest that the distinction between deserving and undeserving residents, already established in the nineteenth century, took on renewed racialized forms in this postwar era and in doing so perpetuated squalor.

In Chapter 5 we turn our focus specifically to the politics and strategies surrounding slum clearances in the postwar era. We pay special attention to the experiences of Black and South Asian residents for whom racism in the housing market oftentimes compelled them to buy or rent in areas considered to be slums. We consider how local government policies effectively destroyed the independence of Black and South Asian families rather than supported independence. In short, we argue that racism forced people into squalor. We then examine a distinct modality of building to replace slums: the "high-rise" tower block. Initially, the high-rise was considered an innovation in habitat that would facilitate social uplift. Influenced by the famous architect Le Corbusier, these tower blocks were vaunted as organic healers of the dysgenic influences emanating from street-level slums. We then track how apprehensions of the high-rise shifted drastically to become akin to nineteenth-century slums – sites that bred criminality and a disorderly communalism.

Chapter 6 turns squarely to the communalism practiced by inner-city youth who inhabited decaying and resource-starved neighbourhoods. By the 1970s, the Black and South Asian presence was presented by populist racists such as Enoch Powell as akin to an invasion force that would turn the white English working class out of their rightfully deserved council homes. We situate the riots and uprisings of the 1970s and 1980s as struggles by marginalized and suppressed youth to defend their locales from fascists, the police and the state. We consider the 1985 uprisings in Broadwater Farm estate in Tottenham, London as exemplary of the way in which architecture, housing policies and racism revealed some of the fundamental fault lines introduced by Margaret Thatcher's revolution in government. In fact, we argue that the oppressive policing of the youth's communalism became the wedge that opened the polity towards neoliberalism.

In Chapter 7 we situate Thatcherism as a qualitative shift in the political struggle over housing policy. In previous chapters we tracked a struggle over the philosophy of housing provision between public good – usually backed by Labour, and private interest – usually promoted by Tories. In this chapter we demonstrate that one of the first battles won by the neoliberal project was over housing. We show how a (Labour-backed) municipal contract between residents and local government was upended by a privatized contract between resident and the market. Substantively, Thatcher's "Right to Buy" initiative radically shifted housing policy from a duty-of-the-state to a right-to-privately-own. We argue that this retreat of the state facilitated a privatizing of risk and safety that led to a new segregation of the enfranchised – those able to comfortably buy into a "property-owning democracy" – from the disenfranchised – those forced to rent privately or service toxic mortgages. This, we argue, provides a key contour of modern-day squalor.

Chapter 8 follows the logics of Thatcher's revolution as they shaped policies under New Labour, specifically public–private partnerships, the outsourcing of a duty of care, and the deregulation of safety standards. Through these modalities we argue that Tony Blair and Gordon Brown led the state to delegate its duty to kill the giant of squalor. We track this "organized negligence" as it

impacted the most vulnerable of society – the homeless and refu-
gees. We then examine the fate of the disenfranchised, who lived
in high-rises and "sink" estates, and with reference to whom New
Labour justified their post-Thatcherite project to establish an
"equality of opportunity". However, we argue that this principle
of equality was pursued through policies that were driven by the
patrician and racializing logics documented in previous chapters.
At the same time, outsourcing and deregulation placed residents
and even homeowners directly in harm's way of flammable and
dangerous building materials. This, too, provides a key contour of
contemporary squalor.

In Chapter 9 we move to the most recent period of British
political history post-financial crisis. We consider how organized
negligence has become even more deadly in a policy era defined
by "austerity". We argue that the Conservative-led governments,
from 2010 onwards, have purified the pursuit of privatization
that had gained speed under New Labour. Conservatives have
now almost entirely redefined "duty of care" as a commitment
to "living within means", while "equality of opportunity" has
been replaced with a fundamental commitment to the interest
of landlords and property as the principal valorizing asset. We
show how in this incredibly unforgiving environment, a push to
privatize housing needs has created a further division between
those who own safe properties that they can financially lever-
age, and those who are burdened with unsafe property that has
increased indebtedness. We then show how riots and uprisings
have been used instrumentally by government to criminalize
residents of estates and receivers of housing welfare to such a
degree that they have even become treated as de facto enemies
of the state.

The concluding chapter turns to the Grenfell Tower fire. We
argue that all the key threads of the book are entangled in the
causes of the fire and the treatment of the residents that suffered. We claim that Grenfell Tower gives us pause to consider

that squalor in the twenty-first century now stalks significant segments of the British population, some of whom would never conceive themselves to be part of such a Dickensian story.

2

A moral history of squalor

The second half of the nineteenth century occupies a particular place in the national imagination. And whilst more contemporary invocations of "Victorian values" seek to return a fractured and transformed polity to a more cohesive and traditional collective past, in truth the Victorian era was also one of fracture and transformation. By the latter half of the century, imperial expansion and industrial urbanization provoked appeals to religion and morality at the same time as they themselves were implicated in the secularization of knowledge – for instance, the new sciences of eugenics and political economy.

Commercial shifts in land use and social hierarchies set the scene for the turbulent Victorian era. Chartering was an eighteenth-century process of establishing corporate ownership through privatizing public land. Enclosure was the process of establishing private property on what had once been communal lands for peasant farmers. By the end of the eighteenth-century, chartering and enclosure had robbed common land from the people, forcing them to dwell more and more in industrial cities in search of work. The landed elites and the mercantile classes who had amassed wealth through industrialism and empire held to a philosophy that their own freedom was bound to their property. They feared the anarchy of the urban poor living in abominable conditions, "masterless men" who had no social standard or

economic investment to bind their energies to. The right to vote
was for the propertied only, the tyranny of the masses had to be
prevented and order imposed upon them.

Many of the chattering classes – those who wrote pamphlets
and discoursed in parliamentary halls, tea houses and private
clubs – saw in the urban poor the prospect of civilizational decline
and a return to "primitive humanity". The poor, they supposed,
lacked a proper work ethic. Self-reliance would have to be their
salvation. To civilize domestic indigents meant to build worthy
habits by destroying corrupting influences, with particular attention to gin – the devil's drink. With horror, the chattering classes
realized that what was commonplace in the colonial periphery
could now be gleaned in the heart of the metropole: encamped
in the slums were a race "apart". No wonder, then, that the term
"squalor" still conjures an image of Dickensian Britain.

In 1794, William Blake wrote a famous poem, "London", in
which he portended about the fate of the city:

> I wander thro' each charter'd street,
> Near where the charter'd Thames does flow.
> And mark in every face I meet
> Marks of weakness, marks of woe.

In 1800, close to the time that Blake wrote, London's population
was 1 million. By 1900, it had grown to 6.7 million as London
became a global city with the world's largest population (a position it held from 1825 until 1914). While many prospered, the
masses did not. Moreover, bad character formation was identified
as a cause of the high birth-rate of the poor, far higher than that of
the middle classes with children often contributing significantly
to the upkeep of the family through paid labour (Pooley 2013).
Divides were becoming cavernous.

As Benjamin Disraeli's novel *Sybil* laid out in 1845, there
increasingly were two nations in Britain – the haves and the have

nots. Disraeli's political philosophy of "one nation" aimed to bind the patricians back to their charges in a way that conserved hierarchies even in the midst of radical change. More progressive ideas of the time held that the worst elements of social life derived not from the nature of humans, but the depredations of their environment. For progressive industrialists such as Robert Owen, the material world's impact on consciousness was primary. Owen therefore believed in the moral salvation of the working class. Yet for Owen, too, this was a patrician's task. The poor had to seek their redemption by following strict rules and regulations wherein cleanliness was paramount and an appropriate separation between animals and humans maintained.

The moral history of squalor that we recount in this chapter exposes the Victorian anxieties and theories that set the path towards twentieth-century social reform. Reformers considered squalor an existential problem not in terms of the humanity of the poor, but in terms of the preservation of the industrial and imperial order. Such populations needed to be embedded back into the body politic in a way that strengthened an orderly hierarchy yet also bred self-reliance all the way down. As the turn of the century neared, these requisites emboldened philanthropists to make of squalor an object of scientific inquiry.

THE RESIDUUM

Before the 1820s, squalor was usually associated with the rural poor. As they travelled from the sticks to the city in search of bread and work, their living conditions attracted more and more attention. Where there was work, there were slums. Ramshackle homes signalled no clear delineation of where one abode ended and another began. With no sanitation epidemics were rife, as was preventable death, at least, given the wealth of the times. Jo in Charles Dickens' *Bleak House* put it best: "Dead, your Majesty. Dead, my lords and gentlemen . . . dying thus around us every day".

Atavistic theories came to forecast a dreaded return to primitive humanity. A concern for civilization itself led to more interventionist ideas.

Sir George Nicholls represents this shift in concern. Nicholls was one of the poor law commissioners who, in the 1834 Poor Law Amendment Act, abolished outdoor poor relief to able-bodied men and their dependents. Subsequently Nicholls moved to London, and in 1854 published the *History of the Poor Law*. In that book, Nicholls (1899: 4) introduced the idea of a "residuum", a small group of individuals who remained in a condition of "primitive poverty, ignorance and subjection" while the rest of the population enjoyed the "higher possibilities of the civilised life". By the 1860s, John Bright, Liberal MP for Birmingham, was deploying the term in parliamentary debate to refer to a small class of men who suffered "almost hopeless poverty and dependence" (Himmelfarb 1966: 126). Social reformers such as Helen Bosanquet also picked up on the term. The "industrial residuum", in her estimation, were a "race who had no specialised skill", only the "minimum of physical strength" (B. Bosanquet & Dendy 1895: 88–9).

Outside of politics and policy proper, public discourse increasingly associated the "residuum" with specific urban locales. Edwin Chadwick's ground-breaking 1842 *Report on the Sanitary Condition of the Labouring Population of Great Britain* connected cholera and other infectious diseases to the "close and overcrowded dwellings" of the "labouring classes", littered with decomposing vegetable and animal matter. For Chadwick (1842: 369), the dysgenic "damp and filth" of such domiciles could be found in both rural villages and larger towns. But before long, other commentators were associating the spread of disease primarily with urban spaces, especially London.

In the late 1840s, and in the midst of the worst cholera epidemic of the nineteenth century, Henry Mayhew, co-founder of the satirical magazine *Punch*, published a series of reports in the *Morning Chronicle*. The series included an investigation of Jacob's

Island, a slum in Bermondsey, London, which just a few years earlier had been seared into middle-class consciousness as the site of Bill Sike's death in Dicken's *Oliver Twist*. Visiting the slum, Mayhew reported that "the air has literally the smell of a graveyard". Later published as *London Labour and the London Poor* (1861), Mayhew sensationalized the residents of slums as beggars, prostitutes and criminals. As we shall see, criminalization of those who live in squalor has been a remarkably persistent feature of social commentary and policy.

At the same time as criminalized, slum-dwellers were also medicalized. That is, their disorderly nature was perceived in terms of the spread of disease. At this point in time, disease was often understood to derive from smell, for example, animal and human excrement. Others believed that disease was caused from a lack of solar energy, which was in scant supply in slums where many homes lacked ventilation and natural sunlight. In any case, the abodes of the lower classes were considered breeding grounds for subcultures that threatened the entire city because with illicit and immoral habits came disease. The cholera epidemics fuelled these worries to feverish levels.

Mayhew's readership, especially the London middle class, would have read his travelogue vicariously, safely ensconced in their orderly and self-contained homes. Indeed, by mid nineteenth century, the capital city's populations were increasingly segregated by class (Jones 1983). Unlike in the rural estates, the bourgeoisie no longer lived close to their paternalistic charges. The topographical distance between master and servant raised similar concerns of "masterless" men as had accompanied the enclosures. What is more, the homes of the poor lay close to the historic centres of the city and, in the minds of chattering classes, threatened the monuments and foundations of their civilization.

Mayhew's tales and others in the genre reported on slum homes as strange counterparts to those of the middle classes (Cuming 2013). Slum living could not easily separate domesticity

and work; many inhabitants carried on trades such as tailoring
and needlework at home. Additionally, many slum dwellings were
built in the alleys and passages meant for horses. These conditions invoked a certain animality that suggested an intimacy with
nature rather than a civilized distance from it. Broken windows,
leaking roofs, poor foundations and outside latrines suggested
that the slum home was open rather than enclosed, thus sharing in the bodily and animal waste that littered the streets. Social
commentary anthropomorphized the habitat of the poor. Their
homes became "dens", "colonies", "rookeries" and even "hovels",
all suggesting animality.

The intimate association between animal and human life was
fundamental to nineteenth-century assessments of the residuum. In 1828 phrenologist George Combe wrote *The Constitution
of Man*, which became a bestseller in the Victorian era. Combe
(2009) argued that society was naturally stratified into three
distinct groups – those in whom animalistic propensities and
instincts dominate (for example, the Irish and criminal classes),
those in whom a balance obtains between animality and the intel-
lect (the majority of society), and those whose intellectual and
moral faculties predominate (the natural leaders). Combe and
others argued that "criminal classes" were simply expressing their
animalistic nature.

The labyrinth-like nature of the slums forbade direct and easy
access to sojourners. These wretched conditions necessarily bred
a sense of counter-community. We shall return to these alternative communalisms later in the book, especially when we examine
modern-day housing estates. For now, though, it is important to
note that authorities and the police often encountered "no go"
areas. The romance of Dickens, as an author, lay in part on his
alleged practice of walking the slums at night.

Although not translated into English until the late nineteenth
century, Friedrich Engel's *The Condition of the Working Class in
England* (1987), published in German in 1845, was amongst the

first to expose the squalor suffered by domestic and migrant workers in the towns and urban areas that housed them. Engels coined the phrase "social murder" to gloss the structural processes that led to premature deaths in England's industrial towns. Considering the fire at Grenfell Tower in 2017, we would argue that the phrase retains its force.

Engel's book is in good part responsible for turning Marx away from philosophy per se and to a materialist analysis of political economy. But Engels did not only attribute the degeneration of workers to material conditions. He was also convinced that the influx of Irish immigrants into slums deculturated English workers. Here, Engels was closer to Combes than Marx. Indeed, domestic industrialization and imperial order conjoined in much of the era's social analyses, even across ideological positions. For example, Thomas Carlyle (1858), a sympathizer of the poor but by no means a revolutionary, argued that the degenerative presence of Irish workers in English towns was cosmic justice for wrongs done across the sea.

The focus on moral, physical and human degeneration speaks to the fact that the idea of a residuum was always a racial one. Commentators seemed to believe that the degeneration of even their own English poor set them apart from – or left behind by – Anglo-Saxon civilization. For instance, the *Saturday Review* presented to its middle-class readership a "caste apart, a race of whom we know nothing" and who occupied particular areas of East London such as Bethnal Green (Malik 1996: 93). Analogies between slums and "primitive" lands also abounded. William Booth (1890), co-founder of the Salvation Army, moralized about "darkest England" thus: "the foul and fetid breath of our slums is almost as poisonous as that of the African swamp. Fever is almost as chronic there as on the Equator."

Stuart Hall (1978: 394), Britain's most influential public intellectual of the twentieth century, once claimed that "race is the modality in which class is lived". Later, we will turn to the political crisis that his pithy phrase sought to understand. For now, though, it might be useful to slightly remix Hall: race is the modality in which squalor is apprehended. That is, the very notion of a residuum references something more than class understood simply as a labour relation of exploitation. Rather, residuum speaks to a dysgenic, discarded, almost-animalistic matter that, due to its continued proximity, contaminates a healthy body politic. This residual could be introduced into an environment as "foreign born", like for instance, the Irish; it could also be "domestic": a discarded portion of the body itself, like the residents of London's docklands or the "cockneys" within audible distance of the Bow bells. When it comes to squalor, class is never innocent of racialized connotations. And for this reason, squalor is perhaps the hardest of all giants to slay.

It is instructive to read these racializing ideologies of the residuum – of animalistic, degenerative, criminal social residue – in commentaries on the London ward of Notting Dale/Barns in North Kensington. Known as "cut-throat alley", the Dale had an association with criminality from very early in its settlement. Issues of security came to the fore when in 1837 the entrepreneur John Whyte built the Kensington Hippodrome, seeking to establish a London racing venue to rival Ascot. Unfortunately for Whyte, the plot of land he leased bordered the Dale. On race days, the locals would cross the fields and watch. As one *Times* correspondent put it "the dirty and dissolute vagabonds of London, a more filthy and disgusting crew" besmirched the events at the Hippodrome. Ultimately Whyte's venture failed. But it left a strong suspicion that the threat deriving from slum residents not only pertained to public health but to the destruction of business ventures by virtue of their mere presence.

By mid-century, one of the principal occupations of the Dale's inhabitants was animal husbandry including pig-fattening. In fact, the slurry from the piggeries was so great that a vast ocean formed in the centre of the area (which later in the century was turned into Avondale Park). Trust Dickens to have an opinion on the matter. The resultant "dirt, filth, and misery", he suggested, "are unsurpassed by anything known even in Ireland", and left residents with shrunken eyes and shrivelled skin (Dickens 1850: 463). In 1864, rather than clear the area, local politicians decided to build a wall around it. In 1893 the *Daily News* reckoned that the Dale was the most "hopelessly degraded" place in London.

The history and geography of the Dale is of great significance to this book, for this is the place that Grenfell Tower was built, then wrapped in a petrol blanket, and burned for the world to see. Notting Dale has always stirred revolt and tension due to the way in which the area places the country's most wealthy in close proximity to some of the country's most destitute. The racialized nature of Notting Dale's segregations and the value judgements that ensue began with Irish gypsies, animal husbandry, and would only be compounded with the arrival of residents from Portugal and Spain, followed then by those from the New Commonwealth – principally, colonies with brown and black majorities which became independent after the Second World War.

A MATRIX OF MOVEMENTS

Fears of contagion and degeneration drove a set of complex and intersecting movements of peoples and transformation of habitats. Many of the fundamental tensions that arose out of these crisscrossing developments in the second half of the nineteenth century have persisted into our own times.

Let us first mention the suburban movement, which began when the wealthy were enticed to take advantage of technological innovations in transportation and remove themselves from the smog filled, crime-ridden and rebellious cities. The building of such sanctuaries increased noticeably after 1840 and continued at a rapid rate until the Second World War. Green and low-density suburban communities were intended to encourage a semi-rural life of family-orientation. However, the first low-density habitations did not succeed in inducing a wider sociality due to a lack of public amenities. Furthermore, many of their designs did not account for growing population, leaving them susceptible to their own forms of urban sprawl as technological changes continued to impact the landscape.

In a parallel movement, a rag-tag development of dwellings emerged alongside railway lines. These suburbs grew up around mills and factories that existed outside cities, while in many instances employers found sites close to existing or intended suburbs. Urban sprawl became a conservation issue, with the satanic mills threatening to infest England's green and pleasant land and spreading the "pestilential masses over [a] much larger surface" (Smith 1989: 108). The landowners of rural Britain began to mobilize against what would henceforth be called "ribbon development".

Still, unless capital was pliable, labour continued to coagulate in the cities. The challenge, then, was to incentivize workers to leave the city and to return to the countryside from which they had been cleared. Much like migrants of the twentieth century, the solution to the residuum was oftentimes presented as "going home". Individuals such as Charles Booth (whom we shall turn to presently) as well as William Beveridge advocated for the unemployed and casually employed city worker and his family to be removed to rural-based labour colonies. A Land Reform Union even advocated for the nationalization of unused rural land on which such colonies could be developed. While a few colonies were set up by charities, the idea never gained significant traction.

What did attract interest and commitment was the creation of new homes in urban or urban-adjacent areas for the respectable labourer. Population movement of this kind was also presented in overtly moralizing terms that tied physical and cultural degeneration to salvation or damnation. Skilled, domiciled and prudential working-class families, the argument went, should be physically distanced from the gin-supping dens where loose morals sullied the nation's soul. As the *Scotsman* put it, to keep "God's poor" around the "devil's poor" was to invite disaster and destruction (Smith 1989: 111). We shall see how this distinction became an abiding one in discussions on squalor, although the terms used would sometimes take on a more scientific gloss.

To enable the repentance of the devil's poor, many liberals of the time subscribed to a philosophy of self-reliance through which even the most downtrodden could reach maturity as free men and husbands. The question remained, though, as to how to induct the poor into this philosophy in a way that did not create the opposite problem of dependence upon philanthropy or state aid. The Charity Organisation Society proposed to walk this fine line between aid and dependency.

Leading the Society was Helen Bosanquet, who we have met already, and Octavia Hill, a celebrated social housing advocate. Like Owen, Hill directly connected the habits and moral character of slum dwellers to their environment. She herself managed various tenements in London, upgraded them from their dilapidated status, and then populated them with the morally suspect poor. Hill's principles as a landlady were to provide clean dwellings, demand their sanitary upkeep, expect prompt payment of rent, and through all this – not quite coercion but "nudging" as we would say nowadays – provide a moral education to her tenants. In fact, Hill claimed that she did not deal with the question of housing alone, but "with houses in connection with their influence on the character and habits of people who inhabit them" (Wohl 1971: 113).

Around the time that Hill was perfecting her system, the first housing development designed for "God's" working-class families was built at London's Shaftesbury Park Estate. The company architect, Robert Austin, planned over 1,000 cottages, with gardens laid out in tree-lined streets to be populated by workers who could afford the rent of between seven and thirteen shillings a week. London's Tottenham was also created for artisans. The two-up, two-down houses of this era were profoundly ideological, seeking to encourage and maintain the nuclear family. In reality, the average occupancy rates across the city suggested that even in "respectable" homes people were often living on top of one another.

Alongside these new philosophies of improvement and habitat designs, slum clearance remained a pressing concern. Crucially, clearance policies were rarely integrated into building policies for new working-class neighbourhoods, and this was a problem that persisted well into the twentieth century. The reason also remains an abiding one: less a movement of social justice, housing reform tended to be a movement of moral paternalism. As such, the key obsession for reformers lay with the undeservedness of slum dwellers (unless proven otherwise) rather than the structural inequalities, segregations and violence that produced and reproduced the differentiation of habitats.

For example, the rents of the new cottages at Shaftesbury Park and elsewhere were not discounted for members of the residuum, who could neither afford to rent nor buy them. Rather than a strategy of equitable provision this was a case of "filtering-up" (see Harris 2012). The strategy was of course deeply flawed. People cleared from slums did not have the financial ability, nor the moral standing to move up but only sideways to streets outside of clearance zones. There, slum conditions would necessarily be reintroduced with houses becoming tenements. Whereupon they would be subdivided as much as was physically possible.

To better understand the deep injustices of slum clearance, we can turn to Edinburgh. In the wake of the Potato Famine, rural Irish workers joined Scottish working-class communities and displaced highlanders in the Old Town of Edinburgh. In 1861, a tenement collapsed killing 35 people. To address overcrowding legislators passed the Edinburgh Improvement Act of 1867, which led to 3,250 families being displaced and only 500 new homes built. The 1867 Act featured the prototype of a "compulsory purchase order" wherein homes were seized at a price the state imposed. Rehousing, inevitably, required land. Planners considered compelling sales from large landowners. In the end, though, land rights and securing the highest return overrode the need to rehouse those cleared. While a right to return was considered, it was never legislated.

Those who planned the Edinburgh clearance presumed that the new homes would provide for the old residents. In actual fact, old residents swelled streets outside of the zone of clearance and merely created new slums in other districts as a response to being displaced. The 1867 Act therefore set a remarkably persistent pattern: when land was needed, it could be taken from the slums where dwellings could simply be levelled, with residents displaced into an equally – or even more – precarious future.

Although dressed in a language of care, the motivations of reformers were paternalistic at best, callous at worst. Moreover, at all times a moral distinction held between those of the working class who reformers believed could be socially uplifted through new housing developments, and those who were undeserving or incapable of such uplift. The history of early slum clearances demonstrates that while considerations of public health were paramount, the livelihoods and security of those dwelling in the cities were not a primary consideration. This moral logic – segregating "God's poor" from the "devil's poor" – shaped and was shaped by economic factors pertaining to land availability and property considerations. In short, a moral economy was complicit in the material transformation of habitat.

TOWARDS A SCIENCE OF SQUALOR

The mood on the streets in the late Victorian period gave the lie to Prime Minister Disraeli's fantasy of "one nation". In February 1886, London experienced riots of unemployed workers who terrorized the well-to-do, sheltering in their horse-drawn carriages. Although order was eventually restored, around 300–400 homeless people continued to camp in Trafalgar Square and St James's Park. As late as November, marches were still being broken up by the police in a brutal fashion. It was during this period that a Liverpool merchant and ship owner called Charles Booth (brother of William Booth) decided to self-finance and direct a survey of the London poor which was to last 17 years.

Booth's survey differed from more sensationalist investigations such as Mayhew's and, while still responding to a perceived moral crisis of destitution, took on a scientific register somewhat represented by Chadwick's earlier report on sanitation. Like Chadwick, Booth was concerned to provide a topography of different habitats. But unlike Chadwick, Booth sketched the city's topography with economic rather than health metrics. For this task, Booth (1897) collected data on occupational status and in doing so divided London's poor into regular workers, irregular workers and the unemployed. Booth then further categorized these populations into four letter grades.

It is fair to say that, for Booth, classes A and B represented the residuum. Class A consisted of a very small number of predominantly vagrant, unemployed and illicit characters, whom Booth classified as "barbarian": a disgrace but not a danger. Class B were the very poor who lived on casual earnings. Although he would later change his mind, Booth initially proposed to physically remove this class from London and place them in labour colonies so that they would not compete with and thus threaten the city livelihoods of classes C and D. For Booth, class C was still improvident, while class D comprised the regular workers who were morally deserving of an adequate standard of living (Brown 1968).

Booth understood the utility of his categorization as enabling the separation of deserving workers from the immoral and dysgenic influence of the undeserving poor. What is more, his categories were formed by "ecological determinism" (Topalov 1993:

415). That is, almost every class was conjoined to the space that it occupied; residents were evaluated in and by their living conditions. In effect, certain residents *became* squalor. Hence, those who populated the Dale, St Giles, and Jacob's Island were painted less as human and more as part of the built environment. Booth's ecological determinism was influential. By 1903, when Helen Bosanquet (1903: 331) returned her attention to the "residuum", she now tied its members exclusively to "a slum or a ghetto or a mean street".

The "scientific" study of squalor, exemplified by Charles Booth, nonetheless built upon the hierarchical and segregating valuation of human worth propounded by the moralistic study of squalor, exemplified by his religious and righteous brother, William Booth. Less a dispassionate paradigm, the science was more a twin to the morality. Nowhere is this clearer than in the way that Britain's late-nineteenth-century imperial fortunes implicated the domestic problem of squalor.

In 1899 tensions in southern African between independent Boer colonies and Britain's Cape Colony boiled over into war. British forces were woefully unprepared for the conflict and the empire only avoided an embarrassing defeat when 60,000 troops, sourced from across the empire, turned the tide. Even though a victory for the British empire, the South African War revealed martial weaknesses at the heart of the imperium. It was widely believed that up to 60 per cent of English volunteers were rejected due to lack of physical fitness (MacKenzie 1976: 515). This shocking prospect meant that empire's integrity increasingly became tied to the putative degeneration of Britain's urban population. Squalor had become as much a geopolitical as a domestic issue.

In 1904, the Inter-Departmental Committee on Physical Deterioration reported from their inquiry into the scandal that "deterioration of certain classes of the population" led to a "sizeable percentage of rejections for physical causes of recruits for the Army". The report (1904: 81) embraced the utility of eugenicist

interventions into population health, with its particular concern for the reproduction of the nation's working-class stock.
On this point, the report argued that urbanization had produced
"consequences prejudicial to the health of the people" and advocated social hygiene policy in terms not only of employment, but
also with regards to housing and environment. Eugenics now
came to accentuate the policy nexus between ideas, morality and
implementation.

In this respect, turn-of-the-century imperial concerns were
addressed, in part, by turn-of-the-century housing reforms based
on ideas that we have canvassed already. For instance, Octavia
Hill's idea of "green belts" – urban-adjacent commons and parks
– was picked up by architect Raymond Unwin who, with Ebenezer Howard, planned the first "garden cities", with construction
of Letchworth beginning in 1903. Their pragmatism led them to
depart from the methodology of the Edinburgh clearances in so
far as they believed that inner-city slums could not be cleared
until more houses were built on the outskirts of the metropole.
Additionally, Unwin was adamant that the largely unplanned
suburban expansion of London had to be controlled with the rein-
troduction of a "proper regard" for "health, convenience or beauty
in the arrangement of the town" (Unwin 2014: 75). Both Howard
and Unwin envisioned working-class autonomy through the construction of garden cities, much influenced by the principles of
Robert Owen. We shall return to these different logics of housing
policy, and their fate, when we interrogate the postwar welfare
state.

In any case, the moral discourses and eugenic ideas of the turn
of the century continued to hold political salience as Britain's
geopolitical position became ever more precarious. In the first
few years of the Second World War, the Hygiene Committee of the
Women's Group on Public Welfare undertook an investigation of
children who had been evacuated from large towns to provincial
smaller locales. The report intentionally drew upon the moral

discourse and eugenic sciences of the *fin de siècle*. The effect of evacuation, noted the writers, "was to flood the dark places with light and bring home to the national consciousness that 'the submerged tenth' described by Charles Booth still exists in our towns, like a hidden sore, poor, dirty, and crude in its habits, an intolerable and degrading burden to decent people" (Women's Group on Public Welfare 1943: xiii). The Committee noted the predominance of "problem families" always on the edge of pauperism and crime, riddled with mental and physical defects. To a nation with a falling birth rate, they calculated, the salvation of every child was more vital than ever.

The intellectual influences tracked in this chapter even reached Beveridge. As a young reformer, he understood the utility of spatial segregation in terms of eugenics, such that social hygiene required good stock to be separated not only from the diseases caused by poor people but by their bad habits and character too. Urban industries tended to produce, in Beveridge's words, a "degenerate posterity" (Harris 2003: 104). Beveridge was first introduced to Charles Booth's work as an undergraduate at Balliol College, Oxford. By 1929, as Director of the London School of Economics, Beveridge had initiated a new survey of London life and labour, with the intent of updating Booth's late-nineteenth-century work. Places and spaces of destitution were where the giants plied their evil crafts.

In sum, by the early twentieth century, housing policy and social reform took on a far more scientific register accompanied by a technical language. Yet, the paternalistic premises and hierarchical logics that informed a moralistic reckoning with the residuum remained. These premises and logics would carry over from philanthropical projects into the state administration of housing – local and national.

3

Housing policy and national reform

The fishing village of Helmsdale was constructed in 1814 to accommodate people displaced in highland clearances and enclosures. Above the town, there stands a memorial featuring flags of Britain's settler colonies. This memorial reminds us that those who suffered the violence of land dispossession at home could, in principle, find benefit in enacting the same processes abroad.

Famous imperialist Cecil Rhodes proposed a solution to the "bread and butter question" by agitating for the acquisition of "new lands for settling the surplus population" of Britain. Indeed, even as the moral crisis of squalor grew across the nineteenth century, Britain was in part able to manage and mitigate the consequences of its unequal development via imperial expansion. In the eight decades after 1850, just under 17 million people emigrated from the British Isles, about 41 per cent of the 1900 population. Yet increasingly, politicians and policymakers sought to undertake social reforms at home. Why the turn around?

David Lloyd George, Chancellor of the Exchequer, led a series of Liberal reforms from 1908 to 1916, which attempted to copy social insurance policies that underpinned Germany's industrial rise to power. Inter-imperial competition gave way to world war and that war cleared the stage for the Russian Revolution. In 1919, Lloyd George, now prime minister, justified an expanded social insurance system by reference to the threat of Bolshevism thus:

"Even if this were to cost hundreds of millions of pounds, what is that to the stability of the state?" (cited in Jones & Murie 2006).

Faced with such a threat to the capitalist system itself, some began to judge the piecemeal voluntaristic character of philanthropic organization as unfit for purpose. Helen Bosanquet and Octavia Hill's Charity Organisation Society was neither sufficiently organized nor nationalized. Thus, early-twentieth-century leaders of industry, politicians and reformers increasingly entertained the prospect that the state might have to be used as a lever for domestic reform. Lloyd George is exemplary of this shift. But even Beveridge considered social reform less in moral terms and more and more through the impersonal metrics of national coordination and planning.

In this chapter we sketch out the late-nineteenth- and early-twentieth-century evolution of domestic housing policy. Concerted state involvement marked a new era in attempts to overcome squalor. However, we will also demonstrate that the premises and practices of nineteenth-century philanthropy – along with their contradictory premises, logics and effects – remained influential.

BUILDING POLITICS

Local administration first began to coherently address housing problems after the Reform Act of 1867, which enfranchised the skilled working class as part of Disraeli's push towards "one nation". In 1869, Liverpool erected the first council housing in the UK (Boughton 2018). In 1880, some 156 council homes were built in Huddersfield's Turnbridge as the local council engaged in a wide programme of municipality. That being said, the first concerted push by local government to build substantial new habitats was undertaken by the London County Council (LCC). Before the First World War, the LCC alone built 10,000 flats and cottages, while all other local authorities combined built between

20,000–30,000 (Wood 1934: 144). London was therefore a concentrated site for innovation in council housing.

The first council housing in London was erected in Shore-
ditch at the turn of the twentieth century. The foundations of the
Boundary Estate were laid on the site of a huge slum clearance. Of
the 5,000 residents cleared to build the Boundary, only 11 found
homes in the new development. In this respect, the estate followed
a logic of segregation established by Charles Booth. The Boundary's red brick, six tenement complex was also built specifically for the deserving working class but not for the residuum.
As Lyndsey Hanley (2007) notes, racial antipathies were built into
housing allocations, as many who were housed on the estate were
Jewish migrants who had settled in London's East End. Displaced
residents moved sideways into neighbouring streets.

The clearances that made way for the Boundary Estate are
indicative of the precarity that planning policies caused in slum
residences. Under the auspices of public health, the Housing of the
Working Classes Act 1885 enabled local authorities to condemn
slum housing without requiring the continuity of provisions for
those who lived there. Five years later, the Housing of the Working Classes Act (1890) qualified this neglect by authorizing local
authorities to use compulsory purchase orders to take over homes
slated for demolition or redevelopment, to pay for the repairs,
maintenance and upkeep of poor stock, and to build homes themselves if necessary. A further revision of the act in 1900 allowed
local authorities to sell what they constructed seven years after
being built if it was deemed unnecessary or too expensive. Even
in its pioneering stage, then, there was clearly an assumption that
council housing was a temporary measure to relieve pressures
that the market could ultimately rectify.

In the previous chapter we examined the relationship between
philanthropists and slum residents. What of the relationship
between local government and the new residents of council
houses?

Although the actual building of council houses was directed by a socially distant – if geographically local – bureaucracy, the administration of these homes rested upon the patrician logics of Victorian social reformers such as Octavia Hill. Provision was made on the grounds that the working poor would learn the virtues of household management. Beyond this, council housing was considered a modality through which to cultivate a political subject that the empire, nation and capital demanded – a patriarchal, prudential, respectable, and industrious working household. Those allocated council housing were expected to socially remove themselves from the vice-ridden, gin-supping scallywags who made the gentry tremble.

The first council homes were not the high-rise tower blocks that we usually associate with this form of habitat. Height was limited to three stories. (Blocks often exceeded this measure but never more than six stories). Planners also favoured garden estates that served as substitutes for England's rural idyll wherein man, animal and nature existed in orderly balance, as opposed to the rookeries, dens, lairs and hovels where man and beast were indistinguishable. As we shall see, the religious nationalism of William Blake evoked by the phrase "green and pleasant land" protected land more than peoples' lives or abodes. The need to limit urbanism and preserve the idylls became a mainstay in twentieth-century housing policies. Instead of frequenting pubs, tenants were encouraged to raise children, take up gardening for self-sustenance and – the height of domesticity – look after pets. Greenery would cultivate the independent and respectful subject that Britain required.

But to be clear, state-induced paternalism had its benefits. The new houses were of a high standard. For the first time, working-class communities were provided with modern amenities – electricity, heating and indoor plumbing. They were also told, categorically, that their tenure was secure.

Glasgow provides a clear example of how this domestic

"civilizing mission" took on an increasingly political significance in the run up to the First World War. Large numbers congregated in the city in expectation of work in the munition factories. Landlords capitalized by inflating rents. Banks raised the rates of their mortgages. Workers rebelled with a rent strike wherein 20,000 people refused to pay their dues. Landlords then moved to prosecute the striking tenants. Only an intervention from David Lloyd George, then Chancellor of the Exchequer, halted the prosecutions. However, before any further legal challenges could be made, the 1915 Rents and Mortgage Interest Restriction Act was passed, which set limits on how much rents and rates of mortgages could be raised. This intervention represented a profound break with the existing order, which rarely pitted property owner against state legislatures.

Historically, war is less a great equalizer and more an instrument of social fracture. The South African War had already raised the political salience of squalor to the level of imperial integrity. During the First World War, the Easter Rebellion in Ireland and the Russian Revolution radically challenged Britain's political conservatism, which, in both its Whig and Tory wings, had proven quite able at containing radicalism. Now, though, state-led social reform was the only response that could be mustered to confront the millenarian promise of communism mixed with national self-determination.

During the end years of the Great War, the Liberal-led coalition government started to scope out a platform of "welfare liberalism" in which the housing problem took on a special significance. In the 1918 general election, Prime Minister Lloyd George committed to a programme of "habitations fit for the heroes that have won the war", condensed by the press to "Homes for Heroes". The prime minister justified the policy of nation-wide council housing thus: "Slums are not fit homes for the men who have won this war. They are not fit nurseries for the children who are to make the Imperial race, and there must be no patching up. This problem has to be undertaken in a way never undertaken before, as a great national charge and duty" (quoted in Pepper & Richmond 2009: 143). Subsequently, the 1919 Housing and Town Planning Act inaugurated a national programme of council housing and slum clearance. Such a politicization of housing nationalized the issue as never before. Prior to 1919, there was no subsidy from central government to remediate the cost of living, and no universal standard of housing. With national legislation, central government funding was allocated to housing provision. Government intervention of this sort was required because of the stark unevenness in the cost of living across cities and regions. After 1919, and empowered by central government, local authorities systematically intervened to build homes. By taking on the costs of building, a local authority could mitigate the costs, or absorb them within the treasury.

Nonetheless, a segregating logic between worthy and unworthy residents was reproduced in national policy, especially in terms of sub-urban versus inner-city development. Land availability was material to this segregation. Local authorities that had green spaces on their peripheries were able to find land relatively easily. In contrast, many inner-city boroughs possessed no usable land and had to either settle for high-density solutions or look to housing people outside of their borders.

The latter policy is what the Corporation of the City of London opted for, which during the interwar years built the most council housing in the country. And most of its activities lay outside what was then the city. This was the era of "Metroland" – the time of ribbon developments, when vast new communities were formed in the likes of Kingsbury, Harrow and the surrounding areas of London stretching to the Chiltern Hills. Between 1870 and the outbreak of the Second World War, the population within Central London declined by 150,000, but Greater London expanded by 1.6 million.

Still, although respectable workers were provided cottages usually outside of the bounds of the city, the residuum remained primarily in their flats and tenements. Neville Chamberlain, chair of the Unhealthy Areas Committee (1919–21), considered flats to be entirely unsuitable for children. Moreover, he argued, the higher blocks were built, the more impractical and expensive they became. In fact, Chamberlain fell into an unlikely alliance with residents of slums.

Take, for instance, the enormous Becontree estate, built in the interwar years for the respectable workers of the East End. Not all of them considered their new estate to be copacetic; some considered it to be a place of exile which separated them from the communities they held ties to. At the very least, many did not want to live in flats. So, representatives for boroughs like Bermondsey argued passionately for the development of cottages for those cleared from the slums, even if no cheap local land existed to build them on.

In the end, the Unhealthy Areas Committee returned to the philosophies of Octavia Hill, arguing against the wholesale clearance of the slums. The Committee instead proposed cyclical repairs and partial demolitions to create more light, at least until the new idylls had been planned and created. Their position was profoundly influenced by Ebenezer Howard and Raymond Unwin, the latter being a member of the Committee. Once again, we can glean here a different logic struggling to articulate housing policy, one that took the needs and opinions of slum-dwellers somewhat seriously. It was not to last.

Before Lloyd George left office, some 176,000 cottages and flats were constructed for the wartime heroes (Wood 1934: 145). But in 1923 a Conservative majority government, led by Stanley Baldwin, put house building back into the hands of the private sector. Chamberlain himself, as Minister of Health, oversaw the 1923 Housing Act which reduced subsidies to local authorities and provided private builders with subsidies. The Act helped the better-off working class to afford their own homes. It left the poorer unaffected. This shift within a national strategy between public control and private provision would be repeated again and again in the post-Second World War era, albeit with diminishing returns for the public good.

That said, Lloyd George's legislative agenda did in some fashion pre-empt the era of the welfare state. Or, at the very least, his agenda elicited many of the tensions and contradictions in house building that would become the staple of politics in the welfare state era. When examined across governments, housing policy was either constructive, destructive or partial – it built, or cleared, or built only for a few. In failing to clear and build synchronously the postwar agenda failed to accommodate all outside of the cultural, economic and ideological cleavages that comprised the working class. Nineteenth-century divisions between God's and the devil's poor had been coded into secular planning policy.

In any case, the legislation introduced in 1919 was only meant to be temporary and to bind local authorities to building council housing until 1927. What is more, the impetus for such legislation was not provided by a desire for structural reform and redistributive justice, but rather by a concern to ameliorate the economic and social disorders caused by the war. The contingencies embedded within social reform would only be resolved after another world war.

A RECKONING

Despite the political contentions and contradictions in housing policy some 4.2 million homes were built in the interwar years. To put these numbers in context: at the outbreak of the Second World War, a third of the whole country's housing stock had been built in mere decades (Becker 1951). The housing industry is even said to have saved the economy from the severity of the Great Depression. Employment figures in the building sector were double those of comparable industries.

During this period, private enterprise outstripped state building by double at its lowest point and by seven times at its peak. Low interest rates, relatively cheap land, a large pool of labour and many other conditions favoured the developers, including the decentralization and relocation of industry. Due to the depression, imports were so cheap that the cost of living is estimated to have declined by 14.5 per cent, with purchasing power increasing by 12 per cent. People could afford to save in ways they could not before and building societies made mortgages more affordable.

Yet, despite the boom in private housing, slum clearance lagged behind. Only 300,000 dwellings were cleared in the interwar period, with the vast majority taking place after 1930 when it was judged that housing stock had been expanded enough to level some homes. The Labour government's Housing Act of 1930 authorized an enormous clearance project, compelling towns and cities of 20,000 residents or more to make plans for slum clearance. The state could buy affected houses at "fair price" and demolish themselves, if necessary. The 1930 Act also set a target for what amounted nationally to 100,000 demolitions per year.

But then the 1933 Housing Act, under the influence of the Conservative government's Minister of Health, Hilton Young, redefined slums with the effect that the state committed to only 12,000 clearances per year. This throttling of clearances remained the case until the outbreak of the Second World War. At the same time, the new Act reversed the commitment from local authorities to build council housing, stipulating instead that local authorities were only to build where the private sector proved inadequate.

Slum clearance dominated discussions of the worst housing, but it was not until 1935 that housing scarcity was addressed legislatively. The state now set standards on how many residents should live per room – two in a one-bedroom, three in a two-bedroom house, and so on. Municipal authorities inspected properties and overcrowding was made a criminal offence with both occupiers and landlords legally bound to prevent overcrowding unless it occurred through "natural family growth". Compounding all these issues was the fact that rents remained prohibitive for the poorest, despite rent controls from the First World War remaining in effect.

If that was not enough, many smaller towns found their industrial base in terminal decline, with needs for copper mining or slate quarrying diminishing. As jobs disappeared, provincial communities began to travel (back) into the cities for work. Complicating these movements was the fact that urban sprawl outwards had put increased strain on the transport infrastructure. Raymond Unwin, who so favoured the decentralization of the cities, held that commuters judged their journeys in "minutes, not miles". This calculation failed, however, when the trains were cancelled and those miles became insurmountable distances.

All in all, the pursuit of housing reform in the interwar years seems to reveal an ever-enlarging assemblage of policy challenges. At the same time, with a Second World War brewing, the governing class could ill afford rebellion. The context required a fundamental reckoning with the ever-increasing need for comprehensive planning at the national level. Labour unrest across the Caribbean led in 1938 to the West India Royal Commission, with Lord Moyne investigating the welfare needs and living standards of colonial subjects. In 1941 the coalition government in Britain set up an inter-departmental committee headed by Beveridge tasked with surveying Britain's social insurance and allied services.

The new war rocked Britain, toppled the French, and all but assured that the United States was to be the dominant economic and military force leading the West. The pace of Germany's industrial rise from the ashes of the First World War, its Blitzkrieg across western Europe, and its narrowly unsuccessful bid on European domination had exposed the short-sightedness of British conservatism. For years, reformers and modernizers had called for industrial investment. The signs were clear that Britain's once pioneering economy was falling behind. Contempt was brewing for the guilty men who had jeopardized Britain's position.

Meanwhile, Keynesian economics gained political traction not simply due to its moral force but also for its practical utility. Keynes brokered lend-lease, formally known as An Act to Promote the Defense of the United States, which provided free aid to Britain, Free France, the Republic of China and eventually the Soviet Union in exchange for military bases to be leased in recipient nations' territory. For Britain, the policy assured a stream of vital supplies from across the Atlantic. The application of this economic policy in peacetime only worked with a huge expansion of American finance postwar. Added to this was the huge economic stimulus provided in the aftermath of the war under the umbrella of Marshall Aid. Both were designed to stem the tide of Bolshevism in Europe. The publication and reception of the Beveridge Report should be contextualised within this era of tumult.

The report has been heralded as the documentary marker of a new era – that of the "welfare state". In fact, the wartime coalition government intended the Commission that Beveridge chaired to undertake a less dramatic task – to investigate the existing system of social insurance, noting where it was falling short so as to adapt it to new needs. Here, the intention was similar to that which drove Lloyd George's reforms at the end of the previous war.

But the popularity of Keynes's arguments for demand-side policies and government intervention, and, above all, the exigencies of the Second World War propelled Beveridge to provide a more audacious plan. Beveridge was all too aware of the social impact of conflict. "Now", he argued, "when the war is abolishing landmarks of every kind [lies] the opportunity to use experience in a clear field. A revolutionary moment in the world's history is a time for revolutions not for patching" (Beveridge 1942: 6). Beveridge conceived of this moment in terms of an attack upon "want" which would be comprehensive in its policy implications, thus battling the other "giants" of disease, ignorance, idleness and squalor.

As had been the case with late-nineteenth-century debates over poverty and its effects, so was Beveridge's report entangled with Britain's shifting geopolitical standing. While the empire's perilous battles in South Africa had previously provided a catalyst for social change, in 1942 it was the Allied victory at el Alamein in North Africa. Widely perceived as a turning point in the war, the victory against the Axis powers was quickly followed by the publication of Beveridge's report. The moment was ripe for radical reform, especially reforms that accepted and adapted to the shifts in the imperium without undermining existing power structures.

Tellingly, before the publication of the report, reconstruction had not been included as an element of British propaganda. But with its publication, the coalition government lost no time in using the report to link reconstruction ambitions to war aims. A shorter version of the report quickly found its way to British troops via the Ministry of Information. By all estimations, the Nazi propaganda machine worried greatly that Beveridge had stolen their principal conceit – that the state should provide for the wellbeing of its (purified) population. By the end of the war, the report stood as an "international testament" as to what governments in peace time might positively do for their long-suffering citizenry (Abel-Smith 1992: 6).

Domestically, the report was just as popular: 635,000 copies were sold. Beyond print, most of the population would have become aware of Beveridge's plan from the profusion of newspapers and magazines that editorialized the report. In February 1943, the report was debated in the House of Commons. Labour accepted the plan and urged for its immediate implementation. The Conservatives were split. Hence, even at this pivotal moment the coalition government managed to agree only in principle to the aims of reform, while balking at some of the details, and delaying implementation until the state of postwar finances were known. Popular cynicism at the government grew, even as the victory over the Axis powers drew closer.

Despite the fact that Beveridge was no expert in housing policy, the politics surrounding the writing and reception of the report implicated squalor in quite profound ways. As early as 1941, a Ministry of Information propaganda piece entitled *Dawn Guard* looked towards the postwar settlement in the aftermath of the "Battle of Britain". Witness one of the two home guards in the film, a working-class man, speculating on social justice: "there must be no more chaps hanging around for work that doesn't come – no more slums neither – no more filthy dirty back streets – no more half-starved kids with no room to play in" (Mackay 2003: 224). The visual accompanying the speech shifts from London back-streets to the leafy suburbs beloved of Raymond Unwin. By 1944, after the report's release, the BBC had begun to broadcast discussions on "homes for all". After wartime bombing of urban areas, survey data suggested that concerns for reconstruction were led by the housing question up until 1947.

THE REPORT: A CONTESTED LEGACY

More than two million homes were damaged or destroyed by the bombing campaign of Germany. The war had flattened buildings in all of Britain's industrial cities. The radical re-imagination of the city valiantly envisaged by the Ministry of Information contrasted with the rubble that urban dwellers navigated daily. If the First World War induced change through fear of rebellion, the Second World War radicalized reform by ravaging cities and mortally wounding the empire.

Squalor was only briefly mentioned in Beveridge's actual report. However, the specific issue of housing put into graphic relief the difficulties of enacting one of Beveridge's key principles of social insurance – adequacy of provision. The Phillips Committee, briefing ministers before the House of Commons debate in 1943, opposed the principle of adequacy arguing that there could be no universal definition of subsistence that captured the geographical and social diversity of living standards. For his part, Beveridge dwelt on the issue of adequacy via a discussion on the "special problem" of rent.

The problem with calculating a universal adequacy of provision was simply that the cost of living was not the same "for all families or in parts of the country". The cause of this difference was in good part due to rents differing "markedly between London, the rest of England and Scotland, and between industrial and agricultural households" (Beveridge 1942: 76). Variability in rents was a crucial issue simply because this particular expenditure, unlike clothing or fuel, was "permanent" and could not be "temporarily interrupted" (Beveridge 1942: 77). Beveridge then admitted that if benefit was to be related to needs, then adjustments to cover the actual rent paid was necessary. Yet he could not quite find a way to adjudicate whether or not above-average rents were reflective of necessity or "wishes" – aspirational or otherwise (Beveridge 1942: 80). And Beveridge certainly did not want to encourage families to live recklessly beyond their means.

In the end, Beveridge argued for a flat rate of insurance contribution that would lead to a flat rate of housing benefit. This resolution, he suggested, had a "strong popular appeal" and would mitigate against charges of unfair treatment (especially vis-à-vis working families) and the creation of dependency upon benefits – an issue that Beveridge had picked up from late-nineteenth-century reformers such as Octavia Hill and Helen Bosanquet. Beveridge admitted that this strategy would not provide for a universal principle of adequacy. Instead, he optimistically hoped that future governments would be successful in their efforts to deal with "urban congestion and shortage of housing" such that inequalities of rents would ultimately disappear (Beveridge 1942: 83).

This avoidance of the fundamental problem of housing provision – inequality and unevenness concretized in the geographies and built environment of the country – is all the more stark if we consider comments that Beveridge made at the opening of the "Rebuilding Britain" exhibition in February 1943, at the time when Parliament was debating his report. Beveridge (1943: 182) was frank to his audience: squalor was not just a "formidable giant" but "harder to attack than Want". In fact, he demonstrated a clear understanding of all the challenges that housing policies had faced in the interwar years. He suggested a national land-use plan, the "sane use" of transport and power to avoid overcrowding, architectural designs that provided for all sanitary amenities within each household, and an efficient building industry that could provide for cheap, plentiful and high-quality houses.

Nevertheless, carefully reading Beveridge's comments reveals a preference for social clearances as a strategy to decongest urban spaces, increase social hygiene, and ensure that only those who needed to live in the city could – and would – do so at their own expense. As a subscriber to eugenicist logics, Beveridge bought into the moral imperative to encourage the reproduction of good working stock and isolate the harmful influences of bad stock.

One can problematize a legacy which places too much emphasis on the Beveridge Report as it pertains to housing. In any case, we would argue that slaying squalor taxed Beveridge's imagination more than any other giant. What is more, we would argue that Beveridge's inability to assure the universal principle of "adequacy" places him in proximity to the late-twentieth-century "wreckers" of the welfare state far more intimately than sanitized renditions of his report might expect.

Take, for instance, the 1985 review of social security embarked upon by the second Thatcher government and promoted as the most substantial review since Beveridge's report. In this review, Norman Fowler, Secretary of State for Social Services, focused in good part on housing benefit as a key means-tested benefit, and one whose provision exemplified Beveridge's own logic that the state should not provide incentives for people to live beyond their means. Fowler recommended the simplification of criteria for determining housing benefit entitlements so that the system would not "undermine incentives to work" thereby addressing the rise of "welfare scroungers" (Phillipson 1984: 99). Beveridge would have sat closer to Fowler than socialists such as Nye Bevan.

But between Beveridge and Thatcher lie some of the most tumultuous decades of housing policy, featuring intense political and economic swings that were at best only presaged in the inter-war period. It is to these decades that we now turn.

4

A postwar consensus?

By the end of the war, Britain's housing situation was in dire straits: 12.5 million homes had been damaged, 250,000 beyond the point of human habitation. Hundreds of thousands more were in desperate need of repairs (Timmins 2001). However, during the war years, house building had been halted. It was no surprise, then, that with a population buoyed by the promises of the Beveridge Report, housing became a cause of militancy across the country. Michael Foot, newly elected MP for Plymouth Devonport and future leader of the Labour Party, recalled that during these years "every MP and every local councillor was being besieged by the endless queue of the homeless" (quoted in Harding 2020: 55).

In 1945, the coalition government presented its Housing White Paper under intense scrutiny. This was the first official document to accept the principle that government should assure that every family could find a dwelling. To discharge such a duty, the government acknowledged that up to four million homes would need to be built immediately. Such acceptance was palatable to Labour, far less so to Conservatives. Nonetheless, having undertaken wartime planning, and having been in a wartime alliance with the Soviet Union, Tories could no longer easily claim that the state was an illegitimate vessel by which to secure public needs.

In 1954, Norman Macrae, a journalist at *The Economist*, coined
the term "Butskellism" – an amalgam of the surnames of then
Conservative Chancellor of the Exchequer R. A. Butler, and his
predecessor, the Labour politician Hugh Gaitskell. Macrae satir-
ically used the term to denote an apparent postwar consensus
between parties when it came to a comprehensive welfare regime,
a mixed economy comprising an alliance between state, business
and labour, and demand management in service of full employment. Butskellism quickly transformed from an amalgam to an
explanatory term, which expanded to include defence policy and
then extended forward to cover the entire period up until Margaret Thatcher's premiership.

In recent years historians have questioned the depth and
strength of this consensus (see Rollings 1996). In this chapter we
demonstrate that, when dealing with the giant of squalor, one
can question whether a consensus ever existed. The same broad
issues confronted politicians and policymakers after the war
as existed before: land allocation, building costs, rent controls,
the moral worth of households, and the segregated and uneven
vista of habitation types. A dissensus emerged over the method
of housing provision as well as the philosophy that underpinned it: a state-controlled provision of general needs versus a
state-supported accommodation of private interests. We shall
argue that if there was any consensus it pertained to underlying
racial hierarchies that informed who should benefit from housing
reform and where.

BEVAN AND POSTWAR BUILDING

The Second World War was incredibly destructive on Britain's
built environment, and any investigation of postwar politics
needs to reckon with the significant needs of the populace for
housing. In 1945, Labour won their first parliamentary majority in
large part due to public fears that postwar reconstruction would

not be taken seriously by the Conservatives. With Labour's victory, the vexed problem of habitation was placed under the remit of the Minister of Health. The task of postwar housing therefore fell upon Aneurin "Nye" Bevan – a name more commonly associated with the creation of the National Health Service.

Bevan's task load in health was intense. It is claimed he often joked that he only had minutes left of his week to attend to housing issues. Yet, if we were to canvas his background, it is reasonable to suppose that Bevan took the challenge of housing with as much seriousness as he did health. Bevan hailed from the valleys of South Wales where the preventable deaths of squalor afflicted his own family. His parents lost five of their ten children before they reached the age of eight. Bevan cut his political teeth in Tredegar – one of those working-class towns that had experienced interwar decline when the ironworks closed in 1931 (see Thomas-Symonds 2015). The interconnection of health and housing would have been political common sense to him.

What Bevan introduced was a profoundly different strategy to the "adequacy of provision" principle that Beveridge and others had debated during the war. Recall that Beveridge admitted to the fact that subsistence costs varied greatly across the country and between classes. But he could not find a mechanism by which to address these disparities such that housing provisions were universally guaranteed. Alternatively, Bevan set about establishing just such universality in what is commonly referred to as a system of "general needs".

This system rested upon two principles of provision – high quality and non-segregation. With regards to the first principle, Bevan significantly increased the footage of homes the state built in his tenure to well in excess of the 1918 Tudor Walters standard of the first national council housing programme. A new three-bedroom home was now 37 per cent larger than those constructed in the late 1930s. These dwellings also enjoyed indoor plumbing, up and downstairs. Bevan was even adamant that building "ugly

things now" would only lead to regret "for the rest or our lives".
His was a modern, futurist vision of British housing.

In terms of the second principle, Bevan departed from previous moral frameworks used by charity organizations as well as
intellectuals such as Beveridge. While not necessarily eschewing
a concern for the dependency-inducing potential of expanded
provisions ("welfarism", as we now refer to it), Bevan did reject the
segregating logic of past policies. He believed it was only through
building mixed communities that the state could right the
wrongs of the past. So, while Bevan might have considered this
mixing in paternalistic terms, he still invoked a cross-class and
cross-occupational community of fate. All elements of society
would live on the same street in a comfortably housed classless
community. This, Bevan said, reflected the way of life of the small
towns he grew up in, where "the doctor, the grocer, the butcher
and the farm labourer all lived in the same street".

Bevan saw the state as uniquely equipped to address the
general need when it came to building quality and solidaristic
habitats. During the interwar period, private interests had constructed 75 per cent of all housing. Bevan sought to reverse the
numbers. He persuaded Edward Dalton, the Chancellor of the
Exchequer, to treble the subsidy for council housing to the effect
that 75 per cent of the payment for new homes would come
from the state's coffers. At the same time, Bevan endeavoured to
strengthen the ability of local authorities to control rents.

Unsurprisingly, Bevan's expansionary programme of state
welfare did not appeal to everyone. The ideological tensions
between Labour and Conservative remained in place during and
after the Second World War. Tories accused Labour of prolonging
the squalid conditions suffered across the country, with Churchill
claiming their policies were driven by "spite" against "free enterprise". Bevan pulled no punches. Speaking in 1946 on how his
housing policy was confounding his critics, Bevan laid out three
areas of redress: the damage from Hitler's bombs, the arrears and

neglect coming from six years of war, and finally "the arrears of housing left by fifty years of Tory misrule in Britain" (Bevan 1946).

As we noted in the preceding chapters, inter-imperial competition had, in various ways, politicized squalor from the late nineteenth century onwards. And geopolitical pressures in no way vanished after 1945. We might think of "austerity" as a phenomenon following the 2008 financial crash. But in fact, Bevan's ambitions ran afoul of austerity too when the United States demanded a tightening of the public purse as a condition of Marshall Aid. By the summer of 1948, parliamentarians were debating whether it was possible to maintain the pace of building.

The progress of reconstruction soon felt glacial in comparison to the immense and enduring need for housing. Beginning in Scunthorpe, then spreading across the country, military installations – some solid, some ramshackle – were squatted by those seeking homes (Hinton 1988). With approximately 40,000 people taking advantage of these wartime habitations, the government could hardly control the situation. After the *Empire Windrush* docked in Tilbury in 1948, many Caribbean citizens found themselves sleeping in Clapham South's deep-level shelter. The turning of the shelter into ad hoc accommodation was facilitated by Baron Baker, an RAF serviceman from Jamaica, who had stayed in London after the end of the war. Baker and those like him were to lay the roots of Ladbroke Grove and Brixton – significant sites in the history of postwar squalor. Here, a new stage of segregation could be identified, evolving in the spaces left over from world war.

PLANNING PROBLEMS

Bevan's ambitions required local authorities to take land if they needed to. The Land Acquisition Act of 1946 greatly increased the efficacy of compulsory purchase orders, an instrument mentioned in the previous chapter. That said, the real expansion of the role of the state came with the New Towns Act of 1946 and Town and Country Planning Act of 1947, both of which made all future developments subject to planning permission, with each local authority statutorily obliged to produce plans for their locality.

In planning terms, there is a process known as "betterment", which pertains to a land value capture mechanism collected via taxation for the benefit of the community (Booth 2012). The ideas behind the 1947 Act were based, in large part, on the ideas of Augustus Uthwatt, who chaired the 1942 Expert Committee on Compensation and Betterment, which had concluded that all of the speculative value added through development should accrue entirely to the state. Uthwatt had, in essence, proposed the nationalization of all future housing developments.

Attlee's Labour government did not go quite so far. Nevertheless, the 1947 Act gave local authorities profound new powers such as requisitioning empty homes and buying land at existing use values. Such powers tackled land speculation and in so doing kept building costs reasonable. The state took 100 per cent of the value produced through development. Landowners received existing use value, not the speculative value deriving from the planned development. Even if they did not like the terms, the sale was compulsory. The state empowered development corporations to purchase the land and plan the developments. Funds collected for this process were deposited in the Central Land Board.

The 1947 Town and Country Planning Act had a significant impact on housing developments outside of large conurbations. The state became the sole provider of planning permission. The shift away from speculative development in the interests of land-owners and developers to a system that publicly pooled the value generated was significant. This move towards redistributive politics at the expense of an accumulative ethos should not be downplayed. Postwar Netherlands and Germany developed similar policies and to this day charge land value capture taxes, which limit the gains of speculative development. However, as we shall see, Britain soon enough pursued a different path.

Nevertheless, behavioural principles remained even in Bevan's system of general needs. No longer uttered only by the philanthropist or expert, now it was state functionaries who most loudly claimed that a "new type of citizen" could be cultivated in new habitats. This was the phrase used by Lewis Silkin, Labour's Minister of Town and Country Planning, as he announced the first ten New Towns in 1946. According to Silkin, these towns would be populated by "healthy, self-respecting, dignified person with a sense of beauty, culture and civic pride" (Smith 2018). As children moved into the New Towns, they were given guides on country life and families were told that they must now respect their neighbours.

To replicate the gentility found in the true "English way of life", as Harlow's master planner Frederick Gibberd put it, and to mark a civilizational distance from city slums, New Towns avoided tower blocks and high-density habitations. Hence, the differences between the New Towns and cities were stark. For instance, the New Towns were planned as low density – 14 people per acre of land; in contrast, various government commissioned reports on city planning accepted densities of 120 per acre or more (Boughton 2018: 95).

Clearly, the New Towns were designed as an alternative to the disorderly communalism of the urban slum and were intended – by both socialist and liberal – to produce a eugenically better stock of worker for a nation recovering from war. The development of the New Towns was itself an extension of the war effort. Tellingly, the development corporations that managed New Towns – dubbed as property developers with a conscience – were generally staffed by retired wartime military officials.

One might consider, then, the extent to which the ethos of New Town development undercut the aspirations for quality, desegregated neighbourhoods which animated Bevan. In practice, getting housed in a New Town was conditional upon finding a job, and the local labour market was generally driven by high-tech industry. The only real exception to the rule were builders, as always. Just how prohibitive New Town housing could be is suggested by a Smithfield Market worker interviewed in a 1986 documentary, *The Making of Modern London*. Seeking to move to Stevenage, this worker claimed that, upon hearing of his profession, the town's authorities told him to go back where he came from: "with me not being skilled, we had no chance" (Taylor 1986).

Just how elitist an affair New Town development could become is suggested by the fact that William Beveridge, now a Lord, was himself head of the Newton Aycliffe development, the first of its kind in the north of England founded in 1947. The site had initially been used in the war as a clandestine munitions factory and the New Town was developed around the existing industry. Beveridge saw Newton Aycliffe as a paradigm of the new social contract. He later moved to the town himself. Every new tenant was vetted and, if accepted, welcomed to the town by the Community Association.

Yet even though a particular class and racial position was fundamental to New Town development, the entire process was driven by the state and underwritten by the Labour Party. For this reason, Conservative commentators apprehended the experiment as a dangerous incubator of socialism. For example, Basildon came to be seen as "Moscow on the Thames", such was the concentrated power of industry and the camaraderie of its workforce. Many in the rich "home counties" also came to resent the legislation, with Stevenage labelled as "Silkingrad" by locals during its development, in opposition to Silkin's accommodation, as Labour minister, of the skilled-working class in Hampshire.

It is, of course, unsurprising that a project seeking to alter the valuation of land would be met with political contestation. Indeed, the Bevan years were taken up with protracted disputes over compensation and struggles over the sale of land. Much of this struggle pertained to ideologies of property. We might rehearse a long history of property rights from the theological reengagement in fifteenth-century imperial Spain with the Thomist tradition of natural law to revisions of classical liberalism by twentieth-century libertarianism perfected by Robert Nozick. Central to these philosophical debates are issues to do with the natural or social origins of land value and by what activities and to whom might value increase and accrue. Along the way, nineteenth-century French philosopher Pierre-Joseph Proudhon best articulated the persistent antipathy and dissent which accompanied struggles between commoner and landowner with his slogan: "property is theft".

In the 1951 election, Tories castigated Labour for building too little. And true, the British housing stock remained woefully unfit for purpose in part due to US-influenced austerity measures. A survey in that year found that 8 million homes were unfit for human habitation, 6 million homes had no indoor toilets, and a fifth of London evinced slum-like conditions. The Conservatives won the right to govern again by promising to provide modern amenities while also committing to build 300,000 homes a year. The new government wasted no time disarming Bevan's housing programme, almost immediately scrapping the New Towns Act. Subsequently, no more New Towns were to be incorporated until the 1960s.

The New Town project has a mixed record. On the one hand, Milton Keynes, developed in the 1970s, represents economic success in providing the highest per capita tax returns outside of London (albeit attracting terms of endearment as varied as "milky beans city of dreams" to "legoland shithole"). On the other hand, and following a familiar pattern, many of the New Towns were constructed around industries that no longer exist. The gendered division of labour baked into the concrete began to buckle as the accommodation of workers in patriarchal domiciles far from the husband's work soon placed severe demands on transport infrastructure. Above all, the New Towns project entrenched the segregation of deserving and undeserving workers within new built environments, despite Bevan's wish to create socio-economically diverse, non-segregated neighbourhoods.

All this, though, was hardly consequential to Tories who had never subscribed to such genial and communitarian aspirations. So, they unrepentantly replaced Labour's housing acts with ad hoc partnership agreements between existing local authorities, whereby those authorities who experienced overcrowding could export their local populations with treasury support. The Conservatives continued to believe that the state was an imperfect mechanism which should only take up the cudgels temporarily when the markets were palpably failing (although by whose determination has always been the sticking point).

No surprise, then, that Tories assumed the level of disrepair in housing stock would be ameliorated if landlords could charge more rent. Despite research projecting a devastating increase in homelessness, evictions and squalor, the Conservative government proceeded to remove wartime controls. The Rent Act of 1957 allowed some of the previously controlled rents to be determined instead by current gross property values. Rents inflated three-fold within the year. Meanwhile, the Conservative government did indeed succeed in fulfilling its election promise of building more "peoples' homes", but only by accepting higher density housing solutions, reducing space standards, and thus, in part, moving away from the principle of general needs.

By 1955, the Conservative government had removed the right of the state – local and national – to requisition homes with all prior requisitions needing to be returned or sold on by 1960. The rights of private property owners, threatened by Labour's commitment to the principle of general needs, were secured once more. Bevan's imprint on housing had effectively been removed.

Such drastic shifts demonstrate that, when it came to planning policies, little political consensus existed in the postwar era. That said, if any consensus did exist between the parties, it concerned migrating members of the New Commonwealth – Black,

Asian, African – and the fear that racial inferiors might undermine the cohesiveness of British society as it rebuilt after the war.

NEW JERUSALEM, NEW RACISM

Even though the British Nationality Act of 1948 rendered all subjects to the crown as British citizens, two years later, the Labour government convened a cabinet committee to consider how the immigration of citizens from the "colonial territories" might be restricted. Even after leaving office in 1951, some Labour MPs continued to express concerns that immigration might put pressure on housing. In 1954, Conservative ministers quizzed labour exchanges as to the worth and character of Black workers and were disturbingly obsessed with the dysgenic and immoral effects of Black men mixing with "white women of the lowest types" (Carter, Harris & Joshi 1987).

However, rebuilding the New Jerusalem, as everyone knew, required the labour power that such immigration provided. In terms of location, the economic needs of Britain placed colonial newcomers principally in the broken cities, amidst the rubble. The new idylls were neither planned nor built with these citizens in mind. New housing was not allocated to Britain's "racial minorities". And even council housing was conditionally allocated on a period of stay. For these reasons, new arrivals found themselves dependent on the vagaries of the private market.

But here, too, discrimination was rife. When it came to buying, house prices were significantly inflated for New Commonwealth buyers compared to their white counterparts. Renting, was no less cruel: this was the era of "no blacks, no dogs, no Irish". In fact, the only people who did not operate with discrimination were slum landlords.

New Commonwealth immigrants formed communities in response to public and private sector racism. They founded informal credit unions and pooled wealth to make mortgage payments.

Additionally, by purchasing property they could rent to members of their own communities. These arrangements usually drew upon existing practices sourced from their places of departure. For instance, Jamaicans used "pardner" and Trinidadians "sou-sou", whereas other groups founded unions through religious networks and kinship (see Sivanandan 1981). More than just financial instruments, these were mechanisms of collective self-help (O'Connell 2011). In a society that denied Black and Asian peoples the ability to manage their own finances and property, creating financial institutions capable of incubating community and realizing owner-occupation was quite a feat.

Nevertheless, such attempts could not easily circumvent bad housing. Black and Asian communities usually had to buy old housing stock in need of repair and in zones that planners had decided to demolish. Furthermore, accommodation was usually overcrowded due to exorbitant costs. For example, many bought houses with seated tenants who were already protected by rent controls, and so mortgage repayments required extra cohabitation. In this context, and given the overheads, material circumstances differed little between owner-occupier and renter.

At this point, it might be useful to once more consider the vexed relationship between race and class. The issue of squalor, though couched in the language of public health, conceals something more than a concern for the lives of those who suffer in the slums. Even before the era of sustained New Commonwealth migration, the urban disenfranchised stood as a "caste apart" who ostensibly threatened the body politic through their loose morals and dysgenic habits. As we noted in Chapter 2, "residuum" was a term that took hold in nineteenth-century politics via an analogical chain of logic that linked the animalistic existence of, for example, the rookeries to colonial primitives. Destitution and impoverishment sullied the nation and blackened the poor. From the nineteenth century onwards, race was always a technology of urban segregation and dispossession.

Still, we should be careful in assuming a smooth and un-changing history of racialization. In the late nineteenth century, eugenic fears of race degeneration were enflamed specifically by inter-imperial wars that were fought overseas. In contrast, after the Second World War, the empire "came home" and racism be-came far more intimate. What is more, however vitriolic the abuse against Irish residents might have been, with a change of surname and elocution lessons, the Celtic "race" could usually pass as Brit-ish. Britain's Black population, to quote Ambalavener Sivanandan (2006: 2), at all times wore their passports on their faces.

Increasingly, the presence of "blacks" and "the pakis" came to be seen as a form of squalor in-and-of-itself. In Chapter 2 we examined how Booth's surveys tended to evaluate the worth of humans via the built environment they occupied. By the 1950s, the built environment was being evaluated via the phenotypes of the humans who lived there. Areas such as St Ann's in Not-tingham, Brixton, Tottenham, Hackney, Peckham, Southall and North Kensington in London, Moss Side and Hulme in Manches-ter (neighbourhoods we shall turn to in the next chapter), Toxteth in Liverpool, St Pauls in Bristol, and Tiger Bay in Cardiff were all tarred with criminality because these were the sites where the new settlers in Britain could lay their roots. To add injury to insult, once settled, new arrivals were then "beaten black" by the "blue" or the fascists.

Let us return to North Kensington once more. After the war, Colin Jordan's White Defence League and Oswald Mosley's fas-cists set up shop in the area, amidst a landscape of bombed out wrecks, stirring despair with racial tensions and pitching the old disenfranchised against the new. Scarcity of jobs and housing was often used in propaganda, as was the presence of Black landlords who were framed as villains. In 1958, North Kensington and St Ann's in Nottingham exploded in racial violence. Both incidents can be traced to a relationship between a white woman and a Black man leading predominately white male crowds to rampage

through the streets in "nigger hunts". For three days, there was
continued unrest in North Kensington, until the Black community rallied and successful chased the racists – or "crazy bal-eds",
to quote Bob Marley – back down the road. It might be noted that
these disturbances in the Dale were a stone's throw from where
the charred remains of Grenfell stand today.

BEHIND RACHMAN

The era of slum landlords is represented in popular memory by
Perec (anglicized to "Peter") Rachman. A Polish refugee, Rachman
developed a property empire around the slums of west and northwest London. However, the rise of Rachman and others of his ilk
was less the result of a few evil individuals and more a consequence of Conservative changes in the administration of housing,
in particular, the shift from state to private provision.

Tellingly, it was not the moral crisis of squalor that shot Rachman to public fame but rather his involvement in the Profumo
affair. For Rachman, too, had had an intimate relationship with
the model Christine Keeler. Thus, not only did the affair implicate
a Conservative cabinet minister within a social circle including
Soviet intelligence agents; it also included slum landlords seeking
to make the most of their investments. This was the limelight in
which Rachman emerged as a mythical figure seeking to exert his
evil influence over state policy.

But let us look behind Rachman's notoriety, whose figure
obfuscates the increasingly racist determinates of squalor in the
postwar era. Consider this: Rachman's properties were rented to
those denied housing due to discrimination elsewhere. Although
remembered as a villain in British history, a Caribbean elder from
Ladbroke Grove strikes a different note: "at least he rented to us".
Incidentally, other people, spaces and places named in the Profumo affair came to be subsequently tarnished, including Frank
Crichlow, a Trinidadian owner of the El Rio Cafe in Notting Hill

frequented by Profumo and Keeler. (Crichlow's story of resilience as he defended his subsequent business the Mangrove from police violence was recently turned into a film in 2020 by Steve McQueen).

Sensational figures such as Rachman hide the fact that there was never a postwar consensus on how to slay the giant of squalor. The struggle between Labour and Conservative policies of land use, property rights, public goods and state intervention puts a question mark over the degree to which "Butskellism" ever united both parties in a governance model based on Keynesianism and welfare provision. The subsequent emergence of Thatcherism is in many ways pre-empted by party differences over the governmental mechanisms by which housing needs could be met. If there was a consensus between parties, then it was far more "Powellite" than we might want to admit. And it is to Enoch Powell's era that we shall now turn.

5

Demolishing slums, building up

Even after two world wars, crumbled city landscapes still largely spoke of a nineteenth-century provenance. Rows of back-to-back terraces built by industry sat next to tenements built for the poor. A window into the appalling nature of living conditions is given by Ron Charnick, a former health inspector in London's Southwark: "Littered with bomb sites, overcrowded, badly damaged, poorly repaired and much unfit housing... Overrun with rats both within and outside public sewers, needing 12 rodent operatives to control. No DDT so infestations of bed bugs, fleas, lice and cockroaches prevalent... Air pollution heavy" (Historia Sanitaria 1954).

Tenants of slum landlords could count on very little regulation or assistance. On those occasions when health inspectors such as Charnick turned up and followed through with enforcements, many landlords abandoned their property, placing the responsibility for the home or its demolition onto the local authority.

In Chapter 2 we noted that Charles Booth's nineteenth-century street survey of London effectively conjoined each class to the space that it occupied such that squalid areas inferred squalid peoples. In Chapter 4 we noted how postwar Commonwealth migration was parsed through the same calculus such that areas populated by Black and Asian peoples were considered squalid due to the racialized demographic. In what now follows we show how a new topography of squalor became integral to the postcolonial political imagination.

In this chapter we examine the politics and strategies of slum clearance in the postwar era, a process that ran parallel to the suburban and New Town building initiatives discussed in the last chapter. We have already noted that slum clearance was always accompanied by a segregation of the working class into "God's" and the "devil's" poor, or, those considered hygienic or dysgenic to the imperial and national project of capital accumulation. However, with New Commonwealth immigration, these segregating logics took on renewed and sharpened racial lines.

Thus far we have argued that social and economic development never followed slum dwellers displaced from their habitats, and so squalor merely reproduced itself down the road. But in this chapter, we turn towards a novel vertical answer to the horizontal reproduction of slums – the high-rise tower block. We situate this new intervention into city planning in the political contexts we sketched out in the previous chapter, including the turn from the principle of universal provision to private property management, and the racialization of New Commonwealth citizens as vectors of squalor.

High-rise tower blocks have long held a notoriety. Britain's cities, especially when compared to their European counterparts, are relatively low density, with the preference for "cottages over flats" determining planning since the moral crisis of squalor came to the fore. As an expedient solution to the problem of the postwar slums, the high-rise on "sink" estates is to contemporary sensibilities what the slums were to Dickensian imaginaries of the rookeries, dens and lairs of the poor. When it happened, the shift in sentiment from the high-rise as a marker of modernity to a stain on the cityscape was sudden and complete. Prince Charles even claimed that the brute concrete architecture of tower blocks had caused more damage to the London skyline than the Luftwaffe.

Alternatively, friends of the poor, such as Neville Chamberlain, were often no advocates for tower blocks. Recall, for instance, his opposition to flats as no place for children or the vulnerable. Given the continued lack of evacuation plans for the most vulnerable, even after Grenfell, it is important to remember that safety concerns accompanied the very first considerations of building high-rises, even given their initial attraction. In what follows we show how Britain's tower blocks, at first considered as a route of social mobility for all denizens of the city, ultimately were denegrated on account of containing and suppressing the postwar postcolonial residuum.

NEW COMMONWEALTH AND NEW CLEARANCES

As part of the Conservative attempt to reposition housing policy away from Nye Bevan's philosophy of general needs, the 1954 Housing Repairs and Rents Act provided mechanisms by which to clear areas of "unfit housing accommodation". Financial Secretary to the Treasury, Henry Brooke MP, provided an update to the House of Commons in 1957, reporting that the number of "unfit houses" closed or demolished had risen from nearly 20,000 in 1954 to about 35,000. While encouraging, Brooke wanted the pace to quicken as council waiting lists continued to grow.

The pace of postwar redevelopment differed between local authorities, but it was in the northwest of England where the challenges were most stark. While in 1945, estimates put 60 per cent of the region's urban housing stock in need of redevelopment, by 1960 27 per cent was considered unfit for habitation (Brown & Cunningham 2016). Manchester's inner-city areas – especially Hulme and Moss Side – held much of the region's worst housing. These were also sites of settlement for African Caribbean and Irish populations.

In the aftermath of the racial violence unleashed in 1958 by white mobs in North Kensington and Nottingham, a racist vernacular of New Commonwealth settlement gained prominence in party politics. In the 1964 general election, Conservative candidate Peter Griffiths engineered what at the time was considered a shock defeat of the Labour incumbent in Smethwick, West Midlands. Supporters of Griffiths platformed the phrase "If you want a nigger for a neighbour, vote Liberal or Labour". Although Griffiths himself did not use the phrase he did not disavow its message. Meanwhile, the local newspaper, the *Smethwick Telephone*, amplified local concerns that Black and Asian settlement would undermine the availability of local housing, inducing immorality, crime and disease (Buettner 2014: 715).

From the South to the Midlands to the North, such racist cartographies were mobilized to make sense of the changing nature of conurbations. In 1966, Granada TV's production *Living On The Edge* presented Manchester's Moss Side as the equivalent of New York's Harlem or LA's Watts district – hotbeds of Black radicalism with a riotous and disorderly potential. Just two years later, Enoch Powell drew upon the same twisted associations when he gave his infamous "Rivers of Blood" speech, which associated the Asian and Black presence with the American Black freedom struggle – meaning, for him, anarchy in the streets and burnt-out businesses and houses.

In racializing the squalor of Moss Side, the actual parameters of the area were stretched by media reports to include parts of Trafford, Longsight, Whalley Range and Hulme – areas that had long held a reputation for criminality and vice. As within many reputations, one might find a strand of truth. After the Street Offences Act of 1959 cleaned up central areas of Manchester, Moss Side did indeed become the primary location for the solicitation of sex work. In point of fact, some of the most notable illicit drinking and gambling establishments were situated opposite Moss Side police station, yet they never faced legal action. Hence, while the deterioration of the area was blamed on an increasing Black populace, the blame should have been apportioned as much if not more to negligent local administration.

In their investigation of Sparkbrook, an inner-city neighbourhood in Birmingham, sociologists John Rex and Robert Moore
(1967) coined the term "zone of transition". Zones such as Sparkbrook and Moss Side were integral to the development of minority
communities who, due to the costs and discriminations faced in
other areas, used less desirable neighbourhoods to anchor themselves and forge connections with fellow sufferers. When it came
to Moss Side, Denmark Road functioned as a central gateway
to the zone of transition. Denmark Road was also located in the
most transitory part of the area, consisting of mostly privately
rented accommodation. It was precisely these zones of transition
that were most affected by the replanning and redevelopment
of Manchester.

Transportation can also be a vector of squalor. The rise in
motorcar use was not factored into early postwar development
policy. As is still evident today, Britain's streets were not suited to
high amounts of traffic, leading to congestions that pollute lungs.
The solution offered in postwar Britain was arterial roads. In fact,
transport redevelopment was a crucial component in the building
of hygienic cityscapes. Yet the placement of these roads revealed
the contempt by which poor and minoritized communities were
often treated.

Let us detour, once again, to Notting Dale, West London.
In 1965, a six-lane flyover was built to ease traffic through Central and West London. When the Westway was built, it split the
North Kensington slums. Compulsory purchases took the homes
of many, regardless of whether they were rented from the likes
of Rachman or self-owned. The development cut through neighbourhoods and blighted the habitat with polluting building
sites that remained in place for years. These developments also
left long-standing blockades and barriers that fundamentally
changed the sense of place and space.

In a similar fashion, Mancunian Way, the first elevated main
road to be built outside of London, cut right through Moss Side

and Hulme. Because census data did not account for ethnicity until the 1990s, it is difficult to be exacting with the numbers. That said, it is reasonably clear that in the 1960s, at the time when projects such as Mancunian Way were put into effect, a significant amount of slum accommodation was Black owned. And local Black activists, such as Ron Phillips, were well aware that this eventuation was all to do with discrimination in council and private housing. This was a situation almost identical to that which attracted New Commonwealth residents to controversial landlords such as Peter Rachman, as outlined in the previous chapter.

When in 1968 plans for slum clearances were announced, it was clear that Moss Side and Hulme were to become the most affected areas. A third of homes slated for destruction were located in Moss Side alone. A Housing Action Group was convened to halt the mass redevelopment and seek out grants for repair instead. By the early 1970s, Phillips argued that Moss Side more closely resembled Belfast than any other part of Britain; at the time of his writing, Belfast had been in the midst of a civil war for eight years.

One would be mistaken for thinking that Moss Side residents enjoyed living in squalid conditions or that they had no abilities or aspirations to live otherwise. Rather, in a racist and classist society, Moss Side became the most promising area in which New Commonwealth residents could build meaningful and self-determining communities. Paradoxically, under the rationale for eradicating squalor, the local authority took the homes of such residents by compulsory order. Even then, payments gave only "bricks and mortar" value, often less than £100, the equivalent of just four months' rent in the new council housing in Hulme.

In any case, some residents stubbornly resisted the plans yet found themselves the only occupier on a cleared street. With little other options, many could only move to new council homes. And so, with a sevenfold increase in social housing occupation over a 20-year period, the area became heavily dependent upon the state. Moss Side was exemplary of the tectonic shifts experienced by Black Mancunians in general. From sourcing housing almost entirely in the private market (rental or ownership), after the slum clearances, 59 per cent of Moss Side residents ended in council housing. Tellingly, those areas where slum clearances were more limited retained higher rates of Black ownership.

Moss Side presents a serious indictment of housing policy. Not only did Black residents lose their homes through slum clearances; they lost their means of independence. But was not Conservative ideology, from Edmund Burke onwards, focused on encouraging orderly independence and reducing disorderly dependency? In whom does the fault of dependency lie?

In Chapter 2 we argued that the moral history of squalor revolved around the idea of a "residuum" – the left behind urban poor who were considered a "caste apart". It is striking to see that in postwar Britain council housing oftentimes became "residualized" through processes of allocation. By the end of the 1960s, Bevan's dream had been torn asunder and two nations were once again emerging in Britain, only this time the horizontal solidarities of class were clearly stratified by the verticality of race. As we shall now show, this sociological crossing had its analogue in the architectural move towards building up.

THE HIGH-RISE

Back in the early twentieth century both Raymond Unwin and the Unhealthy Areas Committee had warned of the need to develop new habitations before destroying old ones. Regardless, past lessons went unlearnt as postwar local authorities struggled to find the space for new developments even as they demolished the old. To finally address this problem, planners turned to the "high-rise", the definition of which is a tower block either of seven-storeys or over or a building that exceeds 18 metres in height. To appreciate the way in which building up was not only an architectural proposition but also a political one, we need to turn to perhaps the most influential – and controversial – architect of the twentieth century, the Swiss-French citizen Charles-Édouard Jeanneret, otherwise known as Le Corbusier.

Le Corbusier's career spanned the world wars as well as the globe. He worked with the French fascist Vichy regime during the Second World War, but also with the United Nations afterwards. He designed buildings and habitats in the USSR, India, France, Japan and the Americas. Le Corbusier's philosophical motivation was based on his claim that if "man" obeyed the laws of nature he would obtain for himself a "conscious sensation of harmony". However, he argued, (and here we find in Le Corbusier a narrative familiar to the nineteenth-century moralizers of the residuum), industrialization had broken man's harmony with nature. When the "tentacled cities were born [Paris, London, New York, Rio de Janeiro, Buenos Aires] ... the countryside was emptied", resulting in a "menacing loss of equilibrium". For this reason, city denizens lived a "disordered and demoralizing existence" (Sutcliffe & Walden 2021).

Le Corbusier presented the purpose of architecture as one of social engineering, that is, to engineer human destiny away from disorder and revolution. Towards this aim, Le Corbusier envisaged urban planning as a way to "naturalize" industrialization. Architectural products would be considered "organisms", and cities organized as if they were biological entities. Organism, for Le Corbusier, was a term that conveyed balance, harmony and symmetry. His philosophy, then, was progressive in the sense of wishing to build over the horrors of squalor, and conservative in the sense that the purpose of the built environment was to neutralize the causes of radical change (whether good or bad).

Over the course of his career, Le Corbusier's designs shifted from ornamentation to large concrete materials which could be constructed quickly in panel systems. His designs sought to construct "streets in the sky", with straight lines, rectangular shapes, and flat roofs. High rises, in Le Corbusier's estimation, could return urban communities to an organic, balanced life once more. His preference for raw concrete – "*béton brut*" in the French – baptised the word "brutalism". The imposing structures led many to see them as brutal unto themselves. This apprehension, though, obfuscated the architectural philosophy that lay behind them.

In Britain, Le Corbusier's influence is hard to measure given that his name is attached – rightly or wrongly – to many of the buildings that define urban Britain, with much of the work maligned as monstrous. Le Corbusier's legacy has even been considered fundamentally anti-British. Still, we should be attentive to the fact that the idea of building up was initially considered, and in accordance with Le Corbusier's beliefs, to be a social good that would extend the ideal of healthy living to all.

Take, for instance, Britain's first tower block built in 1951 in Harlow (a New Town) and named "The Lawn". Although Harlow's master planner, Frederick Gibberd, preferred low builds, it is clear that the Lawn was intended to carry the aesthetic into the sky. Consider the name: there could not have been a clearer reference to the planned organicism of the English country garden and its religious invocation, à la William Blake, of a "green and pleasant land". The Lawn was awarded a Housing Medal from the Ministry of Health. At this point in time, living high off the ground had come to be associated with fresh air and light.

This was a vision far removed from the image of nineteenth-century "rookeries". What is more, supporters of high-rises initially argued that not only did they vastly reduce the costs of land acquisition but allowed more scarce land to be utilized for green spaces. Such arguments led to tower blocks becoming the go-to replacement for inner-city slums. Financial incentives helped. In 1954, legislation was enacted which gave greater subsidies to local authorities the more floors they built on a block.

Again, we remind readers that safety concerns had always accompanied the development of tower blocks, especially when it came to the ability of emergency equipment to reach higher floors. In 1962, the British Standards Institution stipulated in their code of practice for buildings to be "designed so that occupants of floors above a dwelling which is on fire, may, if they choose, remain safely in their own floor". This established the principle of compartmentation, which built with materials and in such a way that a fire could be contained in a dwelling, without the need for evacuating all residents. The code was updated further in 1971, but even here, it merely stated that residents "should" be safe. However, as high-rises were adopted across the country to solve the problem of the slums, the scale of fire safety checks exceeded regulations. Instead of developing a philosophy of enforcement, the state decided to allow building safety to be determined for the most part between the building owner and the insurer. What mattered most to government was the scale of building.

Glasgow's Gorbals is exemplary of the magnitude of the problem that high-rises were supposed to address. The plan to develop the Gorbals entailed a huge clearance of existing populations out of slums that in 1961 were considered the worst in all of Western Europe. The Clyde Valley Regional Plan aimed to decant 250,000 people to New Towns or commuter-belt towns along with industries that would provide jobs. At the same time, planners knew that a significant population would by necessity have to remain in the city. The casualization of labour in certain city industries, particularly in the docks, meant that many areas were populated by the underemployed who had to live in close proximity to their places of work. Hence, a series of high-rise redevelopments were also planned, eventually housing 38 per cent of the previous inhabitants (Grindrod 2014: 152).

In the previous chapter we examined Labour's postwar legislation, which placed the state and local authorities as key arbiters of land allocation, thus diminishing the ability of landowners to earn speculative value from their property. The 1954 legislation that encouraged high-rise building should be considered part of this project. We also noted how the following Conservative government rescinded these political interventions. With the Conservative-authored Land Compensation Act of 1961, the ability of the local state to purchase land at its current use value was essentially brought to an end. Land was to be valued at open market rates.

In later chapters we will attempt to assess the impact of this shift in legislation, especially in terms of how it enabled a comprehensive – and dangerous – financialization of Britain's housing stock in both private and public sectors. Suffice to say, for now, that a recent Housing Communities and Local Government Committee recalls the 1961 Act as enabling "a value reflective of speculative future planning permission" (White 2018). Whereas economist Liam Halligan (2019), hardly a cheerleader of socialism, opines that since the 1961 Act enabled landowners to charge as much as they could get away with, "local authorities have often been forced to compromise on quality, design and density to cope with escalating land prices". Presently, around 61 per cent of the country's wealth is bound up in property (Dorling 2015).

From the vantage point of the present, the 1961 Act was a significant change in the direction of travel. The local state was sanctioned immediately after the war to fulfil the right to houses fit for human habitation. Yet since 1961, local authorities have increasingly managed assets rather than habitation, because land has become a speculative commodity. More than any other act of legislation introduced, land banking derives from the 1961 Act.

Crucially, after 1961 the urban practice of building up became principally driven by the rising cost of land. It was this pecuniary rationale, rather than a grander reharmonization of the social lives of industrial and post-industrial denizens, that drove planning and construction. The 1961 Act perverted the potential of tower blocks to overcome the squalor of slums. In this moment a race–class calculus was fundamental to the reproduction of squalor upwards rather than sideways.

RESIDUUM REDUX

So let us return to Manchester and the fate of its slum clearances. The redevelopment for Hulme comprised both high-rise and low-density buildings. However, and mirroring the move out to New Towns, race and class cleavages determined who would take advantage of which solution. Cottage style housing was taken up by the skilled section of the working class. Alternatively, high-rise estates came to house the so-called "problem families" of Manchester and the recently cleared Black communities of Moss Side. While most council estates were planned at a density of 80 persons per hectare, the new tower blocks had a density of 200 per hectare.

The process whereby resident populations were streamed into low- or high-density housing oftentimes resulted, as we have already suggested, in a forced downward social mobility for Black, Asian and working-class families. Take, for instance, the attempts to gain council housing by those with owner-occupier status. Even if they lived in poverty, even if their homes were being compulsory purchased at a nominal price, social housing providers refused to let anyone of owner-occupier status on their waiting lists. Such refusal even led some previous owner-occupiers into a state of homelessness (Jeffers & Hoggett 1995).

Whether architecture in and of itself bred criminality became a hot topic. In 1972, Oscar Newman, an American architect, wrote *Defensible Space*. The central thesis of this influential book argued that physical layouts of housing estates determined the ability of residents to defend their space. The more communal an area was, the more likely it was to be a crime spot; the more private an area was, the better kept it would be.

Even physical divisions within semi-public spaces created a form of proprietary logics. Newman (1972) claimed that residents who did not privately own a space would still defend it if they knew it was not open to anyone. By this logic, Newman added surveillance to an architecture of segregation, which he insisted was key to reducing crime in large estates. Recall, when it came to slums, the long obsession with visibility and access. Parks, claimed Newman, should be visible from the road, internal corridors should be visible from the outside of a building, and all areas should be well-lit. This was a gospel of one nation under CCTV.

As already noted, after 1961 the rising cost of land became the key driver of large estate building. Architects would often plan for the development of shopping arcades and leisure activities, recognizing, as Le Corbusier did, the need to rebalance and recompose the lives of those living in tower blocks. For instance, influenced by Le Corbusier, the architects of Sheffield's Park Hill estate introduced "deck access" for flats, or what was otherwise called "streets in the sky". Yet due to cost considerations it would often take years for basic shops to establish a presence, let alone libraries or cultural centres. When amenities, congregating spaces and walkways fell into disrepair, as did the future prospects of resident youth, streets in the sky became synonymous with crime.

To understand the political consequences of the post 1961 shift, we need to recall that there lies a subtle ideological difference between invocations of "community" and "communalism". The former speaks to a conservative tradition, going back to the eighteenth-century politician Edmund Burke and his idea of the "little platoons" – patriarchally-led families and village collectives who, while independent, were orderly in their disposition. The latter invokes a kind of collective autonomy that is antithetical to or perverting of established societal norms.

As mentioned in Chapter 2, the off-street nature of nineteenth-century slum housing was presented as animalistic and labyrinth-like, particularly for outsiders and the law. These spaces were considered to have divorced themselves from the public domain, if not humanity per se. In contrast, the advent of on-street housing helped to put in place a "city-scale panopticon" (Severs 2010: 463). Direct and intimate forms of surveillance, it was held, reduced crime and immoral behaviours while making streets accessible to policing. By the time Newman wrote *Defensible Space*, off-street housing had emerged once more, this time in the new estates that effectively blurred public/private divides.

Newman's thesis had a political edge that cut architectural innovations away from the equitable provision of public goods. The high-rise was first embraced as a social and architectural solution to the provision of general need. Now, cost concerns drove high-rise construction and its sociability was pathologized into criminal liability. In short, surveillance was for community and against communalism.

It was not just land costs but building costs that determined the fate of the high-rise project. Large panel system (LPS) construction reached its apogee and nadir in the 1960s when Keith Joseph, then Minister for Housing and Local Government, committed to a programme of building 400,000 new homes in three years. The company responsible for LPS, Taylor Woodrow Anglian, made use of a construction method used for low-lying blocks to build higher. Joseph planned to cut costs by using LPS. Although deriving from a four-story construction method, the LPS system was used to build up to 22 stories wherein precast walls of concrete were made to take all the weight without joint reinforcement.

This system introduced structural weaknesses into high-rises which inevitably revealed themselves in catastrophic fashion. In 1968, an explosion on the 18th floor of Ronan Point tower block in the London Borough of Newham caused a partial collapse killing four people. The Griffiths Report subsequently found evidence of structural defects in the very method of construction and recommended that remedial action be undertaken to strengthen all LPS blocks across the country.

The report was not accepted. Rather, the building industry lobbied tenaciously to provide a method of remediation which they could execute cheaply. For its part, the Ministry of Housing provided guidance that relieved contractors of any obligations to address structural defects beyond basic reinforcements, instead providing two methods to redress the LPS defects. Method A would attend to the joints and defects of construction; method B – the cheaper method – would simply reinforce what could be seen on site. The latter option meant structurally unsound buildings continued to stand. Here we arrive at a history of the present by way of the structural disregard suffered by so many residents of high-rise tower blocks.

Community requires funding. Communalism is the counter-sociability that develops in the absence of funding, security or gainful employment. The illicit nature of communalism's activities should be evaluated as much via a political economy approach as through a lens of criminology. Analyses in the wake of Newman often ignore the importance of shifting access to and provision of resources. Instead, when crime is considered determinative of the building itself, then the actions of residents are considered one-dimensionally as a by-product of poor planning. Regardless, those in positions of power who knowingly execute poor planning are rarely pathologized as criminals.

A CHANGING LANDSCAPE

Even during the period of political handwringing which followed Ronan Point, many LPS blocks continued to be built across the country. Given the history of the Manchester clearances that we have provided, it is easy to guess which segments of the population were considered unworthy to enjoy the basic right to safe housing. Class and race articulated to reproduce squalor in the postwar period as urban habitats were built up. More recently, Danny Dorling (2011) has calculated that the majority of children who live above the fourth floor of high-rises are Black and Asian.

As is always the case when it comes to squalor, the built environment is perceived just as much if not more by the demographic of its inhabitants rather than the materiality of its architecture. As modern building standards have shown, a privately owned block is not necessarily any better built than a public one. At various points in the last century, council homes were built to a better standard than privately built houses. Similar architectural features exist in both private and public housing, and often what is maligned as leading to crime in council or social housing magically transforms into an ornate feature in better-off blocks.

It is now difficult to imagine, in the aftermath of the Grenfell Tower fire, that building up could ever be seen as a modality for social uplift. We do not, however, think about social pathology when we see new apartment buildings hugging the Thames in areas repurposed away from their industrial and/or slum pasts. Until recently, that is. And now we might also note the flammable materials they are wrapped in – an issue that we will return to later.

Before that, we will dwell some more with the youth of inner-city estates and high-rises. It is often the case that this demographic is seen as a problem of squalor – a problem that requires resolution. We will argue, instead, that these youth have sometimes been the most forceful defenders of that audacious postwar housing dream announced by Bevan: to equitably address housing as a general need.

6

The struggle for the city

In 1978, Stuart Hall and a set of co-writers published *Policing the Crisis*, in which they examined the media frenzy over Black "muggings" in the early 1970s. Hall argued that this phenomenon was a manufactured "moral panic". In fact, "mugging" was not a term recognized in British law, but was rather slang imported from the United States, which referenced violent and opportunist robbery, especially of elderly (usually white) women. Hall (1978) was concerned to understand how fear of "black crime" was being mobilized in a political turn towards a "law and order" agenda. Such concerns were to eventuate in specialist police operations, including Operation Trident, run by the Metropolitan Police, which focused in particular on Black violence.

As the Butskellism compromise – such as it was – started to unravel in the 1960s, the prospect of naked class struggle became ever more worrisome to the establishment. Enoch Powell's interventions had built a platform on which to bring the white working class into alliance with business and political leaders in opposition to Black and Asian immigrants who took resources away from "indigenous" working men and, of course, the "traitorous" white elites that defended these newcomer's equal rights. Hall connected such populist developments to the problem of working-class solidarity in times of economic crises.

Hall argued that Black workers were a "sub-proletariat" that lived their class experience through the modality of race. In this respect, a united front of workers could only coalesce if racism was considered by mainstream working-class organizations to be a legitimate injustice for the labour movement. Racism was not just an issue of industrial relations but of class struggle in and of itself. Alternatively, Powell had cast anti-racism as a project that undermined the legitimacy and worthiness of British subjects (worker and elite) at the hands of illegitimate non-white workers and their white elite defenders. By this logic, the moral panic over mugging channelled Powellite politics in times of crises; it was the wedge with which working-class struggle would be blocked.

Of course, mugging was mostly reported to happen in areas that bred "black crime". As we saw in the previous chapter, by the end of the 1960s, slum clearances had become driven by cost concerns rather than by the Bevanite principle of general needs and universal social uplift. Council housing had become the floor from which you could descend no lower, rather than the grounds that prepared you for uplift. Writing in the *Guardian* in 1971, around the time that "mugging" began to take on the feel of a moral panic, Anthony Crosland, previously Labour Secretary of State for Local Government and Regional Planning, admitted that estates had a "whiff of the welfare, of subsidization, of huge [uniformity], and generally of second-class citizenship" (quoted in Reisman 2001: 104).

In this chapter we examine how the economic crises which would inaugurate the Thatcher revolution were accompanied by a series of struggles over what Henri Lefebvre in 1968 called a "right to the city". Similar to Le Corbusier, Lefebvre (1996) considered industrial urbanization detrimental to the human condition. However, Lefebvre focused on the command that capital held over urban life such that its high-density conviviality disintegrated under the pressure of commodification and individualization. And whereas Le Corbusier sought to solve the problem along (small-c) conservative lines, Lefebvre looked towards a revolution inaugurated by city denizens as they took back control from capital and co-created new urban futures.

Nonetheless, as Lester Spence (2016) has suggested, Lefebvre did not quite conceive that the struggles over the right to the city would take place most intensely in those neighbourhoods racialized as dysgenic and unproductive – the locales that the moral panic over mugging indicted. In what follows, we reclaim these struggles as part of the history of squalor. Put another way, we position urban youth in the 1970s and 1980s as leaders in the fight to defeat the giant of squalor.

THE YOUTH REBEL

In Chapter 2, we positioned the late-nineteenth-century moral discourse on squalor within the era's imperial politics, especially the South African War. In the last couple of chapters, we situated the imperial dimension of squalor in a domestic rather than overseas context marked by postwar New Commonwealth migration. Still, we would be remiss to forget the presence of England's first substantive overseas colony – Ireland – even in the new era of postwar "race relations". In Northern Ireland, of course, these imperial legacies were framed principally as religious divides ostensibly mapping onto British or Irish loyalties.

Housing discrimination in Northern Ireland led to the formation of a number of Action Committees seeking redress. The Derry Housing Action Committee (DHAC) formed in 1968 with an aim to root out Rachmanite landlordism and address what they held to be discriminatory practices from the Londonderry Corporation which managed most of the publicly rented properties in the city. Radical direct actions were undertaken such as homeless families squatting disused premises. Meetings were regularly disrupted, and officials heckled. It was through DHAC that the Northern Ireland Civil Rights Association came to organize a march through the city. When this was suppressed, it signalled the beginning of the "Troubles". Bloody Sunday's violence was in part linked to a fight against squalor.

Meanwhile, on the mainland, struggles over the city had to confront the fact that by the early 1970s, even if Britain's imperial power was eclipsing, racism was in the ascendence domestically. At this point in time, New Commonwealth communities in Britain broadly operated under the banner of a "Black politics" which, while not accepted by everyone, spoke to a united front principally between South Asian and Caribbean communities against both the far-right and the racist state. After all, fascist organizing for deportation ran parallel and at times overlapped with a series of legislative acts restricting "coloured immigration". Following the Powell playbook, Thatcher patted the tiger in her run-up to electoral triumph by suggesting that ordinary people in Britain felt swamped by outsiders.

Moreover, for all of the race relations legislation of the 1960s, British law had maintained the right to privately discriminate. Sociologist Ruth Glass put it like this: "as a landlord Mr. Smith can practise discrimination openly; as an employer, he must at least disguise it". Ambalavaner Sivanandan (1981: 112) caught the zeitgeist with his characteristic frankness: "it was their labour that was wanted, not their presence".

The claim that "coloured" residents brought with them physical and cultural contaminants bred a communalism against the racism that had treated the effect as the cause. Struggles against racism were struggles for Black community not only in terms of people but in terms of neighbourhood, even if the built environment was "run-down" or "inner-city" (Prescod 1985). It was also an intergenerational struggle. The children of immigrant parents who had been forced to take up "shit jobs" began to organize frontline resistance for the sake of their own futures. One phrase encapsulated all the various local struggles: "here to stay, here to fight".

Case in point, Southall in West London. Close to Heathrow,

Southall had become a gateway for many South Asian workers driven to the area by factory work. Their children soon found themselves confronting the racism that surrounded and sought to penetrate the community that their parents had built. In 1976, Gurdip Singh Chaggar was stabbed and killed just off Southall Broadway. As he spoke on the murder of a 15-year-old boy, the leader of the National Front, Kingsley Read, proclaimed "One down, one million to go". He was acquitted of inciting racial violence. In response, the Southall Youth Movement was formed, drawing on influences from anti-colonial and anti-racist struggles.

But the movement did not only have to fight the National Front. As was almost always the case, the youth had to fight the police too, some of whom were themselves members of the Front. A "police riot" broke out in Southall on the 23 April 1979. The community had mobilized to prevent the National Front entering the Town Hall. A mass sit-in was planned for 2.00pm in the afternoon. When the youth took to the streets early, 2,756 police went on the attack with the Special Patrol Group leading the charge. They drove their cars down pavements and bludgeoned people in order to create a "sterile area" around the Town Hall. Blair Peach, a teacher from New Zealand, there in solidarity with the Asian community, was struck over the head with an illegal weapon – the blow almost definitely being landed by a member of the Special Patrol Group. He later died from his injuries.

The struggles in West London were mirrored in the East End too – the classical location of squalor. Close to the docks that brought to the metropolis goods and peoples from empire's peripheries, the poor of the area were said to form a "colony" of a "caste apart". Fast forward to the 1970s, and this racialized part of the city now comprised predominantly Bengali men who had migrated ahead of their families and dependents from a politically turbulent country, Bangladesh, that had won an independence war against Pakistan at great cost.

Bengalis lived and worked in terrible conditions, often sharing a bed between two or three people who rotated through shift work. However, for fear that legislation would close the door to immigration, families began to arrive and join the men in an already pressured living environment. Properties in the private rental market were generally overcrowded and incredibly expensive. Meanwhile, Bengali families were usually debarred from council properties. When homes were provided by the local authority, they were often located in estates that had been decanted of their white populations. Alternatively, families partook in the burgeoning squatter movement.

Hence, many Bengali families found themselves living in hostile environments, whether that be poor or precarious housing stock, or with National Front supporters as their neighbours. In response, the Bengal Housing Action Group (BHAG) was stood up to assist families in finding vacant properties in and around Spitalfields and Whitechapel. The acronym for the group translates as "share" or "tiger" in Bengali. This is a fitting double meaning. The women defended the properties from authorities, while young men patrolled their neighbourhoods to ensure community safety from fascist attacks, especially after the killing of Altab Ali in 1978.

The struggles facing the youth is told in the piercing documentary *Blacks Britannica* (Koff 1978). The film was not released upon its completion because the commissioners claimed that it was too hyperbolic. They argued that race relations and class relations were not as dramatic as the film depicted. While battles between producers and executives played out behind closed doors, British streets became riotous as the urban youth rose up. With proof of concept, the film was released in its original form.

Blacks Britannica begins with scholar-activist Colin Prescod arguing that the local state is mobilizing to disrupt the self-organizing of Black communities in areas such as Brixton, Ladbroke Grove, Handsworth and Moss Side. Heavy policing is facilitated by a continual use of the Stop Under Suspicion (SUS) laws. The overriding logic of this intervention, Prescod claims, is to break up the communalism built in so-called "ghettoes". At the same time, negative job prospects for the young generation born or raised in Britain induce a different calculus of living in the "second Babylon" to that of their parents' generation (see also Garrison 1979). (By 1981, the rate of unemployment for black youths aged 16–19 years old was 80 per cent). Thus, the scene is set, Prescod argues, for confrontation between a beefed-up police force and the jobless youth whom British capitalism and the racist state have failed.

On 17 January 1981, Yvonne Ruddock organized a joint birth-day party with her friend Angela Jackson. The party started late, with most people arriving at around midnight. Police then attended due to noise complaints and advised that the windows be closed on the upper floors of the house where the party was being held. At around 5.30am, witnesses reported a white man in a car drive around the house a number of times. A reveller who had left the party recalled seeing a man outside the house vacate a car, which still had the engine running, make a throwing action towards the house, before entering the driver's side of the vehicle, performing a U-turn and fleeing the scene.

The New Cross house fire resulted in the deaths of 13 Black youths aged between 14 and 22. When police considered the possibility of arson, they assumed that the perpetrator had been a disaffected Black party-goer, or that it had been a prank that went wrong. Finally, after consulting forensic expertise, the police claimed that the fire had been self-inflicted, one way or another. Investigators suggested various causes for the fire, for example, a faulty television set, paint thinner, excessive alcohol or cannabis use. By these means the notion of racial animosity as a causal factor was quashed, as was any hope of criminal investigation. The injustice led to the formation of the New Cross Massacre Action Committee which organized a Black People's Day of Action on 2 March in which a 20,000 strong predominantly Black crowd embarked on an eight-hour demonstration winding through central London.

Just one month later, Brixton police launched "Operation Swamp 81", freely wielding the SUS laws and stopping 943 people in just a two-day period. The operation provoked fury. When a black youth was stabbed and the police attended the scene, rumours quickly spread that the police had questioned him first instead of medically assisting him. Police responded by extending the Swamp operation and the Brixton Uprisings began. Some 28 premises were burned down, 56 police vehicles were set alight and hundreds of police injured. In July, the riots and uprisings spread to London's Southall, Birmingham's Handsworth, Liverpool's Toxteth, Leed's Chapeltown and Manchester's Moss Side. In Bradford, 12 members of the United Black Youth League – a splinter group of the Asian Youth League – were indicted for preparing Molotov cocktails with which to defend their community from marauding fascists. All these incidents reveal a frontline defence of precarious living space mounted by marginalized and oppressed youth.

The state responded by appointing Lord Scarman as chair of an inquiry into the causes of the "riots". Scarman approached his subject matter with a governing sensibility not dissimilar to that communicated in Labour's 1975 Housing White Paper. The paper had made the case that it was "vital" to tap the "reservoirs of resilience, initiative and vigour in the racial minority groups and not to allow them to lie unused or to be deflected into negative protest". For his part, Scarman described the racial disadvantages in British society as an "endemic, ineradicable disease threatening the very survival of our society". He also took issue with the decay of the inner cities.

Scarman's report was widely heralded. The report even mainstreamed the premise, now demeaned as "critical race theory", that racism should be examined as a societal condition rather than as individual prejudice. Nonetheless, the language and logic of the report was tinged with Victorian moralism, striking many of the notes of squalor addressed by philanthropists in the nineteenth century. Take, for instance, Scarman's claim that "people are encouraged to secure a stake in, feel a pride in, and have a sense of responsibility for their own area".

This was a classic case of moralizing the problem of squalor such that it was those who suffered from it who had the individual responsibility to change their behaviours. It is worth remembering, and as we documented in the previous chapter, that earlier Conservative housing policies had had the perverse effect of turning independent Black families into dependents of the state. But for Scarman, the riots were not fundamentally the outcome of state policy. Rather, they derived in good part from the pathologies of Black and Asian youth.

More damning was the fact that Scarman buckled under the pressure to absolve the police of wrongdoing, and he declined to accept that institutional racism existed within the force. In analysing the data presented to him to justify the methods used in Swamp 81, Scarman accepted the argument that a higher level of crime naturally existed in Black communities. He presumed that the data drove the policing whereas, in fact, the policing drove the data. In Lambeth, the police created the criminals it believed existed. And so, in opposition to the move made by Stuart Hall in *Policing the Crisis*, Scarman allowed the police to present themselves as the vanguard of moral behaviour.

That said, Scarman did at least point to economic rather than racial determinants of disorder, although even here he did so in the language of individual life-chances rather than via the structures that youth had to navigate. It seemed to Scarman that many Black youth had been given no induction into a working life. Moreover, he noted, there were "few recreational facilities available" and so "the young Black person makes his life the streets and the seedy, commercially-run clubs of Brixton". There, Scarman continued, "he meets criminals, who appear to have no difficulty obtaining the benefits of a materialist society".

Ultimately, the Scarman Report focused on the salvaging of social order. Scarman's institutional response pathologized the communalisms through which the youth sought – imperfectly – to self-determine just futures out of iniquitous pasts. Such a response is to be expected. That said, beyond the resonances with Charles Booth's depiction of slum areas, the report is significant for its acknowledgement that the site of class struggle had moved away from the workplace and into the street. In this respect, the riots and uprisings should be considered fundamentally linked to the struggle over squalor and the battle to slay Beveridge's giants.

BROADWATER FARM

The Broadwater Farm estate in Tottenham provides a lucid case study in how these struggles over the city were neither small nor incoherent but rather magnified and shaped the politics of housing in our contemporary era. Building of Broadwater Farm began in 1965 and was not finished until 1971. But within months of its development, the estate was already being denigrated by the local press as a den of criminality. In the previous chapter we tracked the change in apprehensions over the moral consequences and social utility of high-rises. In the case of Broadwater Farm, its high-rises were depicted not as facilitating upward mobility but rather as reaching new heights of human misery (Severs 2010).

The poor reputation that the estate suffered from at its very inception led to many prospective residents rejecting offers to live there – some 55 per cent. Haringey Council therefore filled the estate with those who had no choice other than to live on the Farm or face homelessness. For this reason 70 per cent of residents were in receipt of benefits, and almost half of occupants were single-parent families – a pathology to the state, who preferred the nuclear family, and also a stick to beat the Black community

over their supposed "absent fathers". The conceit holds that
women à la Beveridge "should, according to common ideology and
state policy" have a man to support them (Pierce 1980: 84). Recall,
also, the moral panic over mugging. Similarly, when it came to
Broadwater Farm, the press race-baited a multiracial youth vis-
à-vis a predominantly white elderly population. Overall, the Farm
was framed through an increasingly populist distinction between
respectable working-class residents versus a semi-criminal (and
heavily racialized) underclass.

A decade after its construction, Broadwater Farm had
attracted such a bad reputation that calls were made to demolish
it. Yet residents on the estate pursued a meaningful life for themselves – as all residents in all built environments tend to do – and
a play group, youth centre and old people's club brought together
the multi-racial population in some kind of convivial fashion
(Sivanandan 1990: 134). This is no surprise since the estate had
been built by architects with the intention of fostering precisely
such a community.

Except that this fostering was increasingly of a communal-
istic kind that, even if a response to injustice, was held in derision
and fear by local administration. At Broadwater Farm, spaces
were opened but away from the street such that the public/
private divide was smudged. The underground car park extended
these spaces in a subterranean fashion. In this environment, those
youth fleeing the police could often lose their predators so long
as they made it to the estate.

Unsurprisingly, the police became highly critical of the estate's
architecture, so much so that measures were taken to henceforth include the force in the planning of large estates. Many of
the estate's residents ended up living under near constant surveillance. Animosity between the police and the estate's youth
intensified despite the actions from residents of the estate to
improve their conditions. When the estate's youth organization
went on a trip to Jamaica, criminals took over the youth centre's

disused shop and started to sell drugs. This was taken as proof that underneath the convivial veneer lay the un-reformable essence of Black criminality.

With no fundamental shift in policing, the antagonisms that led to the conflagrations in 1981 returned in 1985, first in London's Brixton and then in Tottenham's Broadwater Farm. Both eruptions were in response to police incidents. On 28 September, Brixton police searching for Michael Groce in relation to an armed robbery entered his mother's home and shot her. Cherry Groce was paralysed from the waist down; her son was never charged with offences pertaining to the robbery. Then, on 5 October, police raided Cynthia Jarrett's Broadwater home on a groundless charge of theft and assault regarding her son Floyd. The heavy-handed raid caused Jarrett to suffer a heart attack. A demonstration became riotous. In the violence that followed on the estate, PC Keith Blakelock of the Metropolitan Police was hacked to death.

After the death of Blakelock, the police held residents collectively responsible for what happened until the assailants were named to authorities. The police even briefed the prime minister that the community had "acquired napalm" and had stolen a milk float with which to launch a petrol bomb campaign. Stafford Scott, then a senior youth worker, was arrested three times during the investigations but never charged. He sued police successfully. The Broadwater Farm Defence campaign was created when police arrested and charged other young Black men for Blakelock's death. The obsession by the police with Broadwater Farm is revealed by the fact that in 2014 – nearly 30 years after the event – Nicky Jacobs was charged with Blakelock's murder. Once again, the trail failed.

Broadwater Farm had an impact at the political level. Then Home Secretary Douglas Hurd briefed his peers that they "should stand up for police" and proposed the demolition of homes on "difficult estates". Oliver Letwin, an adviser of the Thatcher government, fumed at the idea that the riots should lead to a change in housing policy. Drawing on the populist racism gifted to parliamentary politics by Enoch Powell, Letwin claimed that "lower-class, unemployed white people lived for years in appalling slums without a breakdown of public order on anything like the present scale" (BBC News 2015). There is a whole history of the riot act that Letwin perhaps did not read.

Anyhow, Letwin used moral argumentation to racialize the youth's rebellion, thus separating out God's (white) working class from the devil's (Black) handiwork. "Riots, criminality and social disintegration", he claimed "are caused solely by individual characters and attitudes". Therefore, "so long as bad moral attitudes remain, all efforts to improve the inner cities will founder" (Erlanger 2015). Tellingly, Letwin's own political initiatives ended up focusing less on paternalistic uplift for the chosen few and far more on dismantling housing regulations. In 2017, Letwin was instrumental in launching a Red Tape Initiative that sought to disentangle Britain's post-Brexit regulatory environment from that of the European Union.

In the end, Broadwater Farm received considerable investment and regeneration. Much of the regeneration is to be lauded as it increased quality of life and attended to issues of clear concern to residents, such as flooding. But as part of the regeneration, the large panel system-constructed towers of Broadwater Farm were retrofitted with gas. Less than 20 years after Ronan Point, a London authority was still able to make this error. Yet the most shocking fact of all is that this error was only picked up as part of an increased focus on fire safety following the burning of Grenfell Tower.

AN OPENING FOR NEOLIBERALISM

Between these struggles over the city and the disaster that befell Grenfell Tower lies a series of profound social and economic

revolutions that we now call "neoliberalism" and which drastically affected housing policy. As Stuart Hall put it in the year of
Margaret Thatcher's enthronement as prime minister, neoliberalism impelled a fundamental rearranging of the terrain of class
struggle. Drawing on his analysis in *Policing the Crisis*, Hall (1979)
argued that such a politically consequential rearrangement could
only happen, in the absence of insurrection, through active popular consent to what might be considered authoritarian rule.

We have argued that this popular consent was cultivated in
good part on the racist grounds of segregating the wayward and
dysgenic children of New Commonwealth migrants from a worthy
and deserving indigenous (white) working class. Moreover, these
grounds should be understood in a literal sense: this was a struggle over the built environment, living spaces and neighbourhoods.
By the 1980s, the racist populist wedge that Powell had introduced into party politics pointed towards the council estates
and the pathologies of disorder that their dark and dank corners
cultivated. Before long, not even white residents would escape
the racialization of their habitat. Thus, the end of the twentieth
century took on the moral discourse of the end of the nineteenth
century, with talk of a new residuum – the white underclass.

This is not surprising if we suppose that throughout the
latter half of the twentieth century eugenics remained a science
just under the surface of political rhetoric. And eugenics always
pointed to the same problem in two directions: contamination
from external bodies – the Irish, Blacks, Asians – and internal
bodies – the urban residuum. Letwin, for instance, effectively presented Black estate youth as incapable of uplift and only good for
quarantine. Any attempt, he argued, to refurbish council estates
would only see them "decay through vandalism combined with
neglect; and people will graduate from temporary training or
employment programmes into unemployment or crime" (BBC
News 2015). Letwin also proposed the breaking up of "problem
families" – and these were not all Black or Asian.

In fact, the analysis of such families goes back to Charles Booth and his notion of the "submerged tenth" and, in short, references those whose ability to parent responsibly is called into question. Problem families were identified as a challenge to national fitness in the 1943 report, *Our Towns*, published by the Hygiene Committee of the Women's Group on Public Welfare. As an acting deputy in the Ministry of Health put it in 1946, writing in the *Eugenics Review*, "the general standard of hygiene [of problem families] is lower than that of the animal world" (Wolfinden 1946). In the early 1970s, Keith Joseph, who was not just Minister for Housing but one of the intellectual vanguards of the forthcoming Thatcher revolution, targeted "problem children" in a clearly eugenicist speech (Joseph 1974).

Thatcher fought the 1979 election on three platforms – reducing inflation, tackling the power of the trade unions, and law and order. In her final address before the election, she spoke of peoples' needs to feel "safe in the streets". With victory, the police were given greater powers. Law and order, Thatcher told the country, was not an area she was prepared to economize on. In this war with the "enemy within", she used council housing as a beachhead.

7

The Right to Buy

Running parallel to the struggles over the city was a struggle in the halls of power which pivoted around a redefinition of the very purpose and method of governing. This pivot has been examined through various terms – "neoliberalism", "free enterprise" or "marketization". But all of them reference a principle called "public choice": the market rather than government is the most efficient mechanism by which to maximize social welfare. Part of this principle implies that administrators should govern as if the state – local and national – is a business.

In 1976, Oxford economists Roger Bacon and Walter Eltis published *Britain's Economic Problem: Too Few Producers*. In the book they argued that the growth of government employment was at the expense of capital. They dubbed this swelling of the state as the "British disease" – a "shift of employment from industry to services, and public services in particular". The disease, they argued, "had no equal in any other large Western developed economy" (Bacon & Eltis 1976: 12). As a solution, the authors promoted a pro-business approach, which trusted industry and commerce – rather than the state and administration – with the generation of wealth.

Concerns about state spending pulled at the seams of governance. Many on the Conservative right saw a necessity for huge cuts, using private enterprise to replace state inefficiencies.

As Labour formed a government in the wake of the oil crisis and recession, there was growing acceptance that drastic economic measures would soon need to be taken. Some in government argued that nationalization had not gone far enough. Still, the public mood was shifting as the economy suffered.

Housing and land became key areas of contestation. To reduce costs and generate revenue entailed freeing up and repurposing prime real estate, especially in cities and conurbations. The local state was marshalled to increase the price of land and property as more and more of the nation's wealth became bound to property markets.

The politics of redevelopment from the Edinburgh clearances onwards has always produced dual effects – on the one hand, destroying substandard homes, on the other hand, providing good homes at a higher price. Ruth Glass, a scholar of town planning, presciently described the dual effect that marks our own era of housing policy. "One by one", she wrote in 1964, "many of the working class quarters have been invaded by the middle class ... Once this process of 'gentrification' starts in a district it goes on rapidly until all or most of the working class occupiers are displaced and the whole social character of the district is changed" (Glass 1964: 3, xvii).

The struggle over a new ethos of governing was no less as contentious as the struggles over the city, if less visceral and bloody. But the 1970s was to be the last decade wherein governing parties shifted wildly between public good and private interest. From the 1980s onwards, different platforms for governing came to embrace private interests in housing, such that the claim that housing was a public good diminished in force. This chapter situates the struggles that gave rise to the neoliberal project on the terrain of housing. In this respect, we focus especially on the replacement of a municipal contract between resident and local authority with a privatized contract with the market, otherwise known as the "right to buy".

THE LOCAL COUNCIL AS BATTLEGROUND

Local authorities were effectively created with the Municipal Corporation Act of 1835, and county and district councils were stood up later in the nineteenth century. Bound by and to national legislation, local authorities became crucial nodes in the order of the British polity. From the 1950s onwards, a series of reforms began to transform the local state apparatus (see Cockburn 1977). By the 1960s, American schools of management came to exercise significant influence on such transformations. In 1967, the Maud Committee on the Management of Local Government advanced the idea that councils should be remade in a corporate image.

The Maud Committee recommended the adoption of management boards across all local authorities. Productivity was the watchword of the times and so it seemed only right that business logics should enter municipal structures. The Bains Report of 1972 made similar recommendations as Maud, proposing to replace elite boards with senior management teams. Bains added further weight to the "rationalizing" of services, cutting down committee work and centralizing power. As councils were restructured, much of their work was now commissioned by providers. The local state was slowly being transformed from a municipal provider to a transmission line in a global market of services and goods.

Although Maud did not explicitly recommend the adoption of the title "chief executive" for local authorities, this was the transformative thrust of his argument. By the time that Margaret Thatcher came to power, many local authorities had already dropped the position of Town Clerk – generally occupied by a lawyer – and taken on the "chief executive" in their place – a professional who was often schooled in the business world. McKinsey, a global consultancy firm, began training government on management techniques, channelling the logics of the business world into the discharging of local authority, especially through the watchword of "efficiency", which usually meant saving through cuts.

We often presume the 1970s to be an inevitable prelude to Thatcherism. Yet, in point of fact, and as we made the case for in the previous chapter, this was the start of an era of protracted struggle over the city. In this decade, the fundamentals of housing policy were anything but decided.

It was also a decade in which 40 per cent of Britain's population now lived in council housing. Contrast this with the late nineteenth century, wherein 90 per cent of the population lived in private rental accommodation. Additionally, financial incentives for high-rises had been removed as part of the fallout of the disaster at Ronan Point. In 1969, the General Improvement Areas and Housing Action Areas Act came to replace wholesale clearance zones, with government reverting again to the logics of the 1920s that saw flats as undesirable and land resources for new housing scarce. Low-rise development was once again preferred, for a time.

In some ways, then, at the start of the 1970s the struggle over housing policy was far more contentious than it had ever been in the postwar world. The utility of high-rises was questioned as a cheap means to decant populations without addressing their social uplift. Furthermore, the moralistic ideologies that justified race/class segregations in housing policy were also, at least in part, being challenged in so far as improvement vied with clearance as a policy for remediating substandard housing. This was the conjuncture within which one of the most consequential struggles over housing in Britain took place.

Every struggle has at least two protagonists. Just before Conservative MP Edward Heath became prime minister in the 1970 election, he convened a conference at the Selsdon Park Hotel from which emerged a free-market platform. Included in this platform was a concern for housing. The new Conservative government released a White Paper, "Fair Deal for Housing", which eventuated in the Housing Finance Act of 1972. The Act stopped central government subsidies designed to reduce rents and prevented local authorities from using their rates revenues to subsidize rents.

Those authorities who failed to follow the prescriptions would either lose subsidies for the building of council housing or would have to answer to a housing commissioner sent from central government to enforce the act.

Labour groups from across the country met in Sheffield, voting overwhelmingly to resist the implementation of the bill. Clay Cross, a mining town in North Derbyshire, was especially affected by these new rules considering that over half its population resided in council housing. All local councillors were part of Labour and unanimously rejected the legislation, motioning to resist implementation of the provisions of the new housing Act.

At first, many other councils resisted the Act. Yet, increasing pressure from central government led to most implementing the new policies. Only three local authorities held out until housing commissioners were sent to them; only Clay Cross resisted the commissioners. Councillors were subsequently taken to court for a deficit of nearly £70,000. They were bankrupted and debarred from office. The Labour Party failed to stand by them, despite their committed opposition to the bill on paper. Clay Cross was wiped from the electoral map in the subsequent remaking of local authorities (see Jacobs 1984).

However, industrial unrest and a global economic crisis compounded by OPEC's 1973 oil embargo provided the smallest of openings for Harold Wilson to return to power as a Labour prime minister in 1974. Wilson attempted to roll back Heath's marketization policies and promoted a "social contract" wherein even wages would be nationally controlled. Emboldened by this return to state intervention, a short but significant period emerged with local councillors, generally from the Labour Party, arguing for local state intervention to ensure the continued presence of working-class communities in urban areas.

Such was the hope for a socialist renewal that some commentators predicted the private rental sector would soon wither away entirely. Indeed, Labour's fundamental motivation at this point in

time was to address the inequities of land rights which enabled
speculative wealth to accrue for a few – and only for a few. To end
this injustice, Labour proposed the public ownership of all land
set for development, barring owner-occupied land. Their stated
aim, as Frank Allaun, MP for Salford East later put it, was to "ensure that land was used to meet the living needs of the people and
not just the profits of property speculators" (Hansard 1978).

The Community Land Act of 1975 enabled local authorities
"to acquire, manage and deal with land suitable for development,
and to make other provision for and in connection with the public
ownership of land". This Act sought to return the powers created
in the postwar years by Nye Bevan and stripped by the Tory's Land
Compensation Act. But even in the mid-1970s, the administrative
revolution in local government was advanced. Doreen Massey
(1980: 269), a famous geographer, noted a general complaint that
local authorities were already behaving "little better than property companies".

Regardless, Conservatives fundamentally opposed the Act.
They argued that the state was an agent unfit to allocate and adjudicate housing and land. As evidence, they drew attention to a
£20 million deficit for the taxpayer in the first two years following
the Act. Labour contended that the bill had never been properly
implemented, especially after they had to bend over backwards
with concessions to landowners. Crucially, the Act excluded land
in builders' stocks and land on which planning permission had
already been obtained. This, though, accounted for the majority
of developable land.

Nonetheless, with a number of Acts emboldening state intervention, plus the bursting of a property bubble in the early 1970s,
Wilson's government was still able to create a short but salient
period of municipalization. Through the adoption of improvement schemes, large Georgian houses were bought up by local
authorities and converted into three self-contained flats; in the
absence of such conversions, these properties would no doubt

have been occupied by one professional couple. Given the pressure on public spending, the modernizing of older properties proved a cost-effective alternative to wholesale redevelopment. All in all, Labour municipalized 25,600 homes across the country (Boughton 2018: 165).

Municipal policies helped to maintain a degree of social and ethnic mix in inner-London neighbourhoods that at one time looked as though they might be wholly gentrified. Jerry White, chief executive of the London Borough of Hackney, even suggested that housing tenures might create "a more dynamic, adaptive and tolerant environment than the council estate" (Ellis 2017). Considering the future clashes over Tottenham's Broadwater Farm, this observation marks the path towards a potentially different resolution to the racialized and classed persistence of squalor in postwar – and post-imperial – Britain.

In this respect, the youth rebellions that we described in the previous chapter acted as a bellwether for this protracted struggle over housing and community development. Throughout the 1980s, even as Thatcherism gained hold, central government faced increasing opposition from the local state, particularly in London and Liverpool, where local authorities had incubated what Norman Ginsburg (1979: 7) dubbed "municipal socialism".

Under the leadership of Ken Livingstone (London) and Derek Hatton (Liverpool) the limits of the local state were stretched to breaking point, culminating in the rent-capping rebellion of 1985. Austerity measures were introduced on local authorities, capping their spending significantly, leading to such a shortfall of funds that councils risked breaking their duty of care across numerous services. In a battle very much resembling Clay Cross, Labour authorities from across the country pledged to resist the measures coming from central government, raising rates to make up for budget shortfalls.

The Conservative Party manifesto of 1983 targeted "a number of grossly extravagant Labour authorities whose exorbitant rate demands have caused great distress both to business and domestic ratepayers". Subsequently the government legislated on limitations to rate increases to counter the "high-spending councils". Labour councils then set a collision course with Thatcher. In 1984, Liverpool County Council submitted an "illegal budget" and would not relent until the government provided an extra £20 million for housing, after which it submitted a legal budget. The dispute vindicated resistant approaches to the government and the ripple effect was considerable. Thatcher cast the incident as further evidence of an "enemy within" who, as she put it in her famous speech to the Carlton Club, used "the apparatus of local government to break, defy and subvert the law".

Thatcher won in the end: 18 local authorities were capped for their profligate spending. Those who failed to submit their rates fell into economic crisis. Nationally, the first to collapse their protest was the Greater London Council, despite a campaign from John McDonnell and a minority of Labour councillors who wanted to hold the line. Only Liverpool and Lambeth kept the protest going, and their councillors were duly punished. In total, 81 councillors were charged with wilful misconduct and were required to repay the costs, while being debarred from office.

During this time, the Labour Party fiercely debated whether or not to manoeuvre within the parameters of the law. After a disastrous election campaign in 1983, a new leader, Neil Kinnock, pleaded for a more moderate approach of working within the government-imposed strictures. His saying, "better a dented shield than no shield at all" became the prevailing wisdom of the party. At its 1985 party conference, Kinnock castigated the "Militant Tendency" that had been instrumental to Liverpool's resistance.

A PROPERTY-OWNING DEMOCRACY

Even counting a global contraction in trade, the economic policies of the first Thatcher government were responsible for at least half of all job losses incurred by Britain in the 1980s. To put it bluntly, the Conservatives intentionally de-industrialized the "heartlands". As they did so, unions and the shop steward movement were delivered an almost mortal blow. Instead of Wilson's social contract between wage earners and business, Thatcher offered another compact: a property-owning democracy.

Back in 1924, the originator of the phrase, Conservative MP Noel Skelton, had in mind something quite different: workers co-owning the businesses that they were employed in. Thatcher, though, reached back further to ideas of liberty inherent in the right to own private property and the orderly independence that patri-archal inheritance induced in the body politic, à la Edmund Burke. Her use of the term was evident even in the Conservative response to Labour's 1975 Community Land Bill. There, the opposition announced their belief in the "superiority of a nationwide property-owning democracy over the collectivist concept of community land". If municipal socialism sought to construct the new citizen via state intervention, Thatcher did so through the Right to Buy.

The attempt by Thatcher's government to clear the field for this property-owning democracy was of a quality different to other previous Conservative attempts at reforming land politics and housing policies. And to understand the project that this new citizen was mobilized to support, we must first appreciate the importance of land and property to Thatcher's revolution.

With deindustrialization, the new avenues for profitability were crafted by financialization. Firms shifted business models away from production via long-term investment towards making money from short-term speculative trade in financial commodities. With Thatcher, land politics were marketized primarily – but not exclusively – through property.

Prior to council housing and the development of public parks, the state did not own any land. Only the Crown did, and its land, as Brett Christophers (2019) shows, has never been "public". However, by the late twentieth century, local authorities had come to own a lot of the urban landscape. Privately developing that land generally came with the promise of work because developments led to jobs and houses. Yet with the privatization of land there was generally an increase in land-hoarding, which developed less of a property-owning democracy and more of a rentier economy, servicing an affluent, landowning elite.

Christophers (2019) presents this pivotal moment with dramatic figures. Following Thatcher's opening up of the state's land to markets, the British state has sold approximately 2 million hectares – 10 per cent of the entire British land mass. Some 20 per cent of this land was sold as part of the privatization of British industry, with the remaining 80 per cent sold as land qua land. This amounts to approximately £400 billion in today's prices. While Right to Buy is often presented as the largest privatization of the era, it was land's privatization that eclipsed all others and enabled housing to be so captured by financialization. The effect has been momentous, as Danny Dorling (2015) notes: "housing prices in the UK rose sixfold from 1983 to 2007, but land prices increased sixteenfold".

Within days of her first election, Margaret Thatcher's government set out the details of the Right to Buy policy. Within a year, the 1980 Housing Act came into effect, enabling tenants of at least three years residence to buy their council house at a 33 per cent discount to the market price, with a 44 per cent discount for flats. The Act raised somewhere between £22 and £28 billion before Thatcher left office and generated more capital than the privatization of gas, electric and British Telecom combined (see Timmins 2001; Boughton 2018).

The Right to Buy was pitched in populist terms as an empowering mechanism for the deserving populous who had been failed

by a bloated and interfering state. In the best tradition of housing policy, the Right to Buy took on overtones of self-reliance and
other moral characteristics so often imputed into God's deserving
poor. For example, Michael Heseltine, then Secretary of State for
the Environment, believed that the policy would achieve "independence from the State, among our citizens" (Begley 2020). The
Right to Buy fundamentally shifted the terrain of struggle, so
vividly mapped out on urban streets. We might even say that it
was a policy designed in part to stem Black and Asian bolshevism.

But to be clear: the Right to Buy was an incredibly popular
policy. Polling in the late 1970s showed 60–70 per cent approval
ratings for the sale of council homes. Council estates, with their
uniformity and stigmatization, were not exactly desirable; but
making a home your own still appealed. What is more, the notion
of a right to buy did not, historically, owe only to one party. Even
local Labour councillors had, in the 1950s, offered tenants the
chance to buy houses that were being bought up by local authorities. Additionally, Thatcher had originally opposed the Right to
Buy, believing it to be unfair to those who bought on the private
housing market. So, the Right to Buy was, in some sense, a gram-
mar shared between parties.

The difference was that Thatcher embraced the policy with
gusto once she realized how it might forward her ambition to fundamentally shift the relationship citizens had with their state. In
fact, housing was the arena in which Thatcher believed she could
most easily break "the culture of dependency". She abandoned the
original idea that money generated from sales would be invested
into building for the most vulnerable tenants. Local councils were
instead pressured to use the proceeds to reduce their own debts.
Then the threshold for taking advantage of the Right to Buy was
dropped to two years and the maximum subsidy raised to 60 per
cent later in the decade (70 per cent for flats).

The results were impressive, if stark. State spending on housing in the first five years of Right to Buy reduced by over £2 billion.

Housing development halved. By 1982, building levels were at their lowest since the Second World War. Renovations and municipal initiatives also declined significantly. Between 1979 and 1994, total public expenditure on housing fell in real terms by 60 per cent. The manufacturing of scarcity when it came to affordable and accessible housing is an abiding legacy of the Right to Buy. Contemporary squalor owes, in good part, to this pivotal moment in what came to be known as the neoliberal revolution.

The vast majority of the homes purchased under Right to Buy were either houses or low-rise flats which had been built to a good standard. Flats in high-rises were particularly hard to sell, which led to further incentives and reductions applied to them. A glimpse of what was to come later is provided by London's Wandsworth Council, which purchased a whole tower block for a relatively small price and refurbished it for a prospective young professional class. However, many council-run tower blocks during the Thatcher years entered into a spiral of decay, obsolescence and neglect. This portion of housing stock was not insignificant, comprising 440,000 flats mostly in city centres. During this time period, the stigma attached to estates deepened, with local administrations treating them almost solely as a financial burden and seedbeds of criminality.

And so, the government set about transferring large estates to voluntary organizations. This transferal programme was a crucial corollary of the Right to Buy, because the "Tenants Choice" programme opened up council housing to financialization. Subsequently, some of the country's most neglected estates were taken under the administration of Housing Action Trusts (HATs), who renovated, remediated and securitized before transferring ownership away from the local council.

Housing Associations were the preferred choice, but the move towards arms-length management organizations (ALMOs), which was fully sanctioned under New Labour, had its seeds sown in 1988. Owned by the local authority, an ALMO is a management organization that separates the role of landlord from strategic housing concerns. ALMOs, like housing associations, are nominally non-profit. Both organizations can commercially manage properties for profit, although their structure precludes shareholders and the corporatism of the private sector. The use of ALMOs was spearheaded by Conservative local authorities in the south of England. By 1994 such authorities had transferred the homes of half a million tenants into housing associations.

With the Housing Act of 1988, any large housing project had to be administered through a housing association. Associations were thus given access to private sector finance for public projects. Or, more accurately, associations were required to fundraise privately to supplement public money for new builds, furthering the marketization of housing needs. This was an opening of seismic proportions, streaming private capital into public projects, and transforming the welfare state into a market socitey. Above all, the interest on private loans incurred by housing associations was too high to afford the subsidization of good housing necessary to meet the needs of the poorest, including those at threat from homelessness. Increasingly, this demographic was transferred sideways into large estates, with even these habitats being run (down) by associations instead of local authorities. The press then dubbed such estates "welfare ghettos".

The introduction of financialization into council provision of housing once more produced an abiding geography in which squalor was recomposed. The Right to Buy destroyed municipalization and the possibility of providing general need on equitable grounds. Financialization ultimately won the struggle for the city. A new wedge was driven into social housing that again sorted out God's charges from the devil's: the working class enfranchised into a new national compact via house and low-rise flat property ownership versus a disenfranchised, low earning "underclass" who remained residing in estates without exercising their right to property. The right to the city, à la Lefebvre, was not just

questioned but effectively criminalized. The only legitimate right
was a right to buy.

THE BEGINNINGS OF ORGANIZED NEGLIGENCE

Integral to Thatcher's new model of growth was the private rental
sector which, however, initially declined due to the Right to Buy
programme. In response, government removed rent controls
from all new lettings (albeit also adding some new protections
for tenants). Further stimulation of the market came in 1988
with tax breaks offered to institutions and private investors who
would build homes for rent. Tenants of private rentals were especially disadvantaged by the 1988 Housing Act, which, barring a
few exceptions, allowed landlords to evict any occupant for any
reason with only two months' notice. In 1989, Norman Ginsburg
(1989: 60), a social policy expert, dubbed the government's policies "Rachmanism with tax breaks".

After seemingly fated to oblivion in the 1970s, the private
rental market emerged from the 1980s fully resurrected. Those
in the decaying inner cities found that, despite the squalor they
faced and the violence they experienced on their streets, they
were living on speculative goldmines. A new will to remove the
struggling working class and unemployed out of the city consoli-
dated as the price of land continued to rise.

But that is not all. At the same time, the drive to deregulate the
housing sector would see the government cut building regulations
from more than 300 pages to just 25. Fire safety was weakened
considerably, with no formal requirement to ensure buildings
were "deemed to satisfy" the remaining regulations. The government justified the short cut on the grounds that compliance was
a "significant financial burden" (Review of Fire Policy, presented
to Parliament 26 June 1980). In removing and revoking controls
the government knew there was a danger of enabling the conditions for multiple frequent fires. They therefore sought to cut only

so deep that deregulation would not lead to an "unacceptable increase in loss of property or casualties" (Fire Brigades Union 2019: 19).

Dangers faced the newly enfranchised property-owning working class too. In 1985 the Thatcher government opened up previously unavailable lines of credit to the working class. That household indebtedness had the potential to turn toxic was not considered by those in Thatcher's orbit, who trusted instead that home owners would comfortably attach themselves to a political conservatism. Ever increasing inflation of assets would paradoxically create a new dependence upon financial markets. The credit crunch of 2008 was foretold in the housing market collapse of the late 1980s and early 1990s. As council housing diminished, unintentional homelessness increased significantly, tripling between 1979 and 1991.

Yet despite all these tectonic shifts Thatcher had only begun a revolution in government. Upon her taking office, there existed 5.1 million council homes; upon her leaving office, 3.7 million still remained (Timmins 2001). Privatization, financialization, outsourcing and deregulation formed a toxic brew that enriched some at the expense of throwing many into increasingly precarious living conditions – financially and materially. Thatcher had brought the ingredients together, but the process had just started under her rule, especially considering how high-rise estates remained deeply undesirable to many of her new property-holding subjects – albeit not for too much longer. That said, with the introduction of Right to Buy we can identify the causes of a squalor peculiar to our own era – what might be called an organized negligence by the state of the housing sector.

8

Organized negligence

Previously we noted that Friedrich Engels used the term "social murder" to describe premature deaths amongst urban workers caused by industrialization. Engels might be forgiven for rhetorical excess. However, the structural violence his term implies has a long tradition of analysis in Marxist political economy.

In 1982, geographer David Harvey published *The Limits to Capital*. In seeking to understand the process of urbanization within a capitalist context, Harvey wished to update some of the basic explanations of capitalism provided by Karl Marx. For our purposes, the book is important due to its attempt to think through how mobile circuits of capital shape and affect built environments and neighbourhoods. Harvey (1982: 397) described part of this process as an "organized abandonment" of locales by capital.

Harvey took an example of organized abandonment from his then place of residence, Baltimore. "Redlining" refers to a historical practice of using covenants to exclude Black people from owning property in planned neighbourhoods. Redlining can also take more subtle racist forms, such as denying – or massively increasing the cost of – financial services for people living in a particular postcode that just so happens to be predominantly populated by Black people. Harvey's point was that this abandonment of the neighbourhood by finance was anything but haphazard. Rather it was organized via institutions that had mastery over the transmission line from local populations through the state to capital. Organized abandonment is almost always poverty-inducing and, in short, maintains destitution and therefore squalor.

Another geographer, Ruth Wilson Gilmore, mainly known nowadays for her work on prison abolition, updated Harvey's thoughts in the 2000s to refer to neoliberal state reorganization specifically. Glossing many of the processes that we described in the previous two chapters, Gilmore (2008) connects organized abandonment to crisis-led restructurings of the economy. More recently, Brenna Bhandar (2018), a critical legal theorist, has used the term "organized state abandonment" to describe the conditions that led to the Grenfell Tower fire. Bhandar speaks incisively of the "abandonment of the state's responsibilities" to provide safety and security for its citizenry, noting how such abandonment reignites hostility towards the poor and working class, as well as more recently arrived migrants.

Throughout the twentieth century we have tracked a political modulation between public-focused and private-leading policies pertaining to local and national planning, building and administration of housing. We have seen how this modulation generated policies designed to defeat squalor and in some cases was instrumental in the reformation of squalor. Even on the eve of Thatcher's election victory, the modulation between public and private remained strong: municipalism presented a viable path to resolve the struggle over the city. Yet, after the Right to Buy revolution, this modulation was significantly weakened – and to the benefit of capital. For instance, public–private partnerships, perfected during New Labour, did not seek to diminish private interests for the public good, but rather tied public duties to the modalities of private interests.

Writing this book five years after the Grenfell Tower fire, and in light of the evidence produced since, it has become clearer to us, at least, that there was no abandonment of the residents. Rather, public duties were outsourced to private providers, and their administration deregulated in the same movement, so as to create a structural – rather than random or mistaken – neglect of the Tower's residents. If abandoned, a community is free to determine their own rules of conduct. Negligence is more pernicious. A neglected community remains trapped in rules that do not serve their interests or even provide for their basic safety.

In this chapter, we track the evolution of organized negligence through the Blair years by following the fate of the vulnerable – homeless and asylum seekers – as well as the despised and criminalized – especially Muslim communities and estate youth. We connect outsourcing to the dangerous deregulation that led to the Grenfell Tower fire. Organized negligence, we contend, is the form that twenty-first-century squalor takes on.

THE VULNERABLE

The organized neglect of those most vulnerable to housing needs is best understood by examining the changing fortunes of the homeless and asylum seekers during the neoliberal era. We mentioned in the previous chapter that the financialization of house buying led to dangers even for those who took advantage of the Right to Buy. In 1983, as part of its attempt to encourage home ownership, the government introduced a mortgage interest relief at source programme (MIRAS) that used the treasury to subsidize private ownership by almost £8 billion. Sure enough, though, recessions during the late eighties and early nineties led to thousands of home repossessions. As people lost their homes, they slid down the social scales, often finding themselves in the private rental sector dependent upon benefits. Nearly 150,000 people were officially registered as homeless in 1991, triple the numbers in 1979. The unregistered homeless were doubtlessly far more numerous, as 40 per cent of applicants were rejected (Smith 1995).

The difference pre- and post-Thatcher can be gleaned from the reception of Ken Loach's 1966 film, *Cathy Come Home*. The film portrayed a family struggling in a system without the statutory right to a home. Cathy is separated from her partner Reg, before having her children taken into the care system. The film suggests that, left to the discretion of the local authority, injustices could emerge through the caprice of council officers. The film sent shockwaves through Britain, leading to the formation of a number of homeless charities, housing associations such as the Notting Hill Housing Trust, and eventually the 1977 Homeless Persons Act which made the local state responsible for housing the most vulnerable.

The 1977 act was novel. Nothing like it had existed before. The act proposed a very broad definition of homelessness which in many ways significantly undercut the Victorian moralities that assigned blame to the character of the suffering individual. If people were not at fault and could no longer live in their current conditions, then it was a duty of the local state to provide a permanent home. The partiality of the council authorities often led to protracted disputes, and resolutions only worked through the same council, compounding issues of discrimination. Nevertheless, for many who were statutorily housed, it was a lifeline.

But with a diminution of council housing caused by the Right to Buy, and faced with rising homelessness, John Major's government "effectively tore up" the 1977 Act (Hodkinson & Robbins 2013: 62). Permanent accommodation was replaced with temporary accommodations including hostels or supported living spaces that were increasingly outsourced. The criteria for homelessness were narrowed considerably, moving away from a standard of reasonable need and instead focusing on a notion of "rootlessness" – i.e., living on the street.

The 1996 Housing Act also barred asylum seekers and irregular migrants from being eligible for assistance if they could be said to be occupying any accommodation, however temporary. Indeed, the organized negligence of homeless people and asylum seekers proceeded in parallel. Britain's refugee and asylum-seeking population grew considerably in the late 1980s and 1990s due to wars in Europe, Africa and the Middle East. The press reportage settled on the lowest common Powellite denominator and warned of yet another existential threat to British values. Not only that, but this xenophobic logic was also mobilized as part of neoliberal designs. Shock stories in the media, particularly the Murdoch press, painted pictures of lives of luxury for those housed in the capital. The value of the asset was framed as liquid wealth, the market value of an asylum-seeker's shelter trumped their legal entitlements as humans.

When it comes to xenophobia, Labour and Conservative governments tend to enjoy consensus. The Conservative-authored 1993 Asylum and Immigration Appeals Act recused local authorities from a duty to house asylum seekers on a permanent basis. Pending the resolution of their status, asylum seekers had no freedom of movement. Then, in 1999, the New Labour government penned an Immigration and Asylum Act which repealed the provisions of the 1948 National Assistance Act for persons "subject to immigration control", i.e. asylum seekers. New Labour further centralized the administration of asylum seekers within the Home Office, which promptly outsourced the task to a "consortia".

More and more stories abounded in the British media that asylum seekers were taking up scarce council housing. The response, formalized under New Labour, was designed to pacify the new middle classes who now voted for the red rose. It was simple: house those made destitute by war in the poorest regions of the country. Asylum accommodation was often identifiable due to the use of same colour doors or drapes. Predictably, racist attacks occurred on asylum seekers with some even eventuating in murder. "Soon enough", as Arun Kundnani (2007: 85) notes, "Home Office planners were ... drawing up lists of towns where the racism had reached such a pitch that no more asylum seekers could be sent there".

All this, though, was in good part caused by the deepening of organized negligence. Local authorities had already suffered significant diminution of their housing stock to the detriment of *all* vulnerable people. Furthermore, deindustrialized areas suffered reduced house prices, which encouraged enterprising landlords to buy and convert properties into accommodation for the most vulnerable, but at significant additional cost to local authorities that were already having to make savings for "efficiency's sake".

The gain to private landlords was accompanied by an outsourcing of administration. For instance, the formation of initial accommodation reception centres was entirely contracted out to global security companies such as G4S and Serco. Even today, some of the most vulnerable and marginalized people reside in these centres. They are arguably some of the worst sites of squalor in modern Britain. And despite the regularity of fines being administered to these institutions, the outsourced role of the private sector in such a core aspect of statehood has yet to be seriously rethought.

THE DESPISED AND CRIMINALIZED

Financial deregulation allowed for the creation of low interest buy-to-let mortgages. The rapidly expanding buy-to-let market, in turn, supercharged the private letting agency sector. Discriminations in this sector were far more pervasive than in the public sector and oftentimes far more quotidian. For instance, postings which did not accept applicants on housing benefit discriminated against the poor in general. Paradoxically, at the same time, and because of the state's purposeful swelling of the private sector, the housing benefit bill inflated from £800 million to £4 billion in little over a decade. This was further exacerbated by steep increases in council rents, which had tripled over the course of the 1980s.

Recall Nye Bevan's principle of general needs. Every successful attack on this principle led to more and more scarcity in council housing. This manufactured scarcity fed into Powellite arguments concerning who the truly deserving working class was. The "replacement theories" of fascism spread in areas such as Barking. There, the British National Party (BNP) argued that immigrants should not be allowed to "go to the front of the queue". Instead, they insisted that length of residency should be considered in housing allocations in order to preserve the whiteness of the area. The BNP even argued that (white) families should be compelled to pass their tenancies onto their children.

Under Nick Griffin's leadership in the early 2000s, the BNP began to win local council seats, capitalizing on urban unrest that shook New Labour even at the start of its tenure. In the summer of 2001, the National Front stoked fires across the northwest of England, marching through Oldham first, then Burnley, and working their way to Bradford. Labour's Home Secretary David Blunkett banned the march. However, South Asian members of the Bradford community who had got word that the National Front were meeting in a pub went to confront them. One man was stabbed. Riots ensued. Some 187 people were charged. They received what was at the time the most severe legal punishment for rioting in British history.

New Labour's decision to join the US wars in Afghanistan and Iraq following the 9/11 attacks further inflamed issues. A war on terror logic entered domestic life predicated upon an obsession with Islamic alterity. Media and public discussions abounded over the existential threat posed by a growth in Arab, North African and Somali British communities. When the allegiances of these communities were questioned, so was their right to remain in council housing.

Figures such as Abu Hamza, the "hate preacher" from Finsbury Park Mosque, stood in for ordinary residents in Bradford, Burnley and Birmingham. (Hamza had brought up his family in a house estimated to be worth well in excess of £1 million.) Housing was once more debated as a lever of behavioural change, as it had been in Octavia Hill's days. Calls to revoke the tenancies of those who did not pass a narrow standard of assimilation increased. All this put electoral pressure on New Labour. By 2007, Margaret Hodge, Minister of State for Industry and the Regions, felt it necessary to concede that British families had a "legitimate sense of entitlement" over immigrants. Arguably, these tensions fed into Brexit debates less than ten years later.

But to repeat a point we made earlier: the root of the problem did not lie in racial demography but rather in political economy. Religion was far less consequential to "community cohesion" than the radical reduction in council housing stock, council funding and revenue, and widespread un- or underemployment. Masked behind a convenient politics of nativism was an unwillingness to tackle the key driver of social dislocation in the 1990s and 2000s: the ever-inflating price of land and housing. The financialization of housing had created a mutant giant, arguably harder to slay than ever before.

During the 2000s, increasing numbers of individuals and families found themselves stuck in a "rent trap". Over-priced rentals denuded residents of the ability to save up for a low rung on the housing ladder. Still, they were perhaps the luckier quintile. Meanwhile, the deregulation of the rental sector and the increasing reliance on private landlords to house the most vulnerable led to such scarcity that enterprising landlords converted sheds into accommodation.

More recently, houses that would have been cleared at an earlier time in British history have now become second-tier stock for second-tier citizens. That is, houses previously planned for demolition, once local government funding was withdrawn then became housing for asylum seekers. For understandable reasons, many asylum seekers attempt to house themselves rather than live in squalid conditions, dependent on vouchers. Between 2006 and 2016, the government estimated that concealed households doubled leading to 2.5 million living in overcrowded conditions. Currently, entire families live in single rooms or sheds converted into homes. London's undocumented population is purportedly the size of Sheffield. It is sobering to think that it is now routine for thermal imaging drones and planes to monitor the suburbs of London for illegal shack dwellings alongside cannabis farms.

What, then, of those estates made notorious in the 1980s as sites of disorderly people and criminal habits? When Labour took power, the Chartered Institute for Housing estimated that the backlog of repairs to council stock was in the realm of £10 billion. Many estates had in fact entered a process of "managed decline" – an outcome of organized negligence – with underfunded and threadbare councils unable to fund the necessary upkeep and remediation. Ventilation suffered, concrete bred mould, lifts and intercoms broke, and pipes leaked. It is not surprising that the cultural form most associated with the estates in the last 20 years is called Grime (see Charles 2016).

In June 1997 Tony Blair gave his inaugural speech as prime minister on precisely one of these sites. The Aylesbury Estate was completed in 1977, with 2,700 flats providing housing for up to 10,000 people. Over the course of two decades, conditions on the estate had deteriorated. Blair took this backdrop to be the mission of New Labour: to provide an equality of opportunity to the "forgotten people" of the Thatcher years whose life chances had been arrested.

Recalling Nye Bevan, Blair regretted that "all that is left of the high hopes of the postwar planners is derelict concrete". Nonetheless, his speech evoked the familiar figure of "problem families". Blair conjured households "three generations" deep in unemployment, save for the "drugs industry". In a separate radio address, Blair described estates such as Aylesbury as "sinking ships", hence the phrase "sink estate". As Jess Perera (2019) notes, sinking also connotes a process that we can connect back to ideas of dysgenic environments and degenerated peoples, i.e. the residuum of old. Except that now, it was a multiracial "underclass" full of "problem families" who needed to be salvaged by a new Labour mission.

It is of course true that, with a loss of jobs and widespread unemployment, criminal avenues were taken by many of the youth whom Thatcher and her fellows had experimented upon. Heroin and crack cocaine came to afflict great damage on neighbourhoods across the country, breaking up families and encouraging petty theft to feed addictions. Crack singularly contributed to the evisceration of a social-justice oriented communalism and left behind a sense of sketchiness: anything could and did happen. The effect that drugs had on certain areas was a form of squalor unto itself. The drug trade dominated certain social geographies. Streets were littered with the trade's detritus – crack vials and used needles. Communities that had once been synonymous with resistance and culture became notorious for drug related crimes. The ease of access to drugs made such localities prime sites for gentrification, with young professionals gravitating toward a "vibrant" nightlife.

For all the pomp and ceremony, and over £56 million through the New Deals for Communities programme, the Aylesbury Estate is now set for total demolition with a net loss of 931 socially rented homes. One might say that first they come for the drugs, then they take the homes. Or, as the satire of the young professionals taking over *Being a Dickhead's Cool* so eruditely summed it up: "I remember when the kids at school would call me names, now we are taking over their estates". The hipsters create the demand, the police criminalize the suppliers and a cycle conducive to clearance emerges. To quote Perera (2019: 22): "Policing in London today is being organized around the project of regenerating London and in turn, gentrifying it".

With the Crime and Disorder Act of 1998, New Labour updated SUS laws by reference to the highly influential "broken windows" theory of Republican Mayor of New York Rudi Giuliani (he of Trump fame). The theory claimed that adopting harsh and draconian sentences for petty acts of vandalism would discourage individuals to commit serious crime. Effectively, the theory updated Oscar Newman's 1970s argument for defensible space, which posited that the more communal an area was, the more likely it was to be a crime spot. And who occupied communal areas on estates more than any other demographic? The youth, of course, who, in the best tradition of rustic idealism, did indeed wish to breath fresh air.

Hence, petty crimes were met with antisocial behaviour orders (ASBOs), which could be served to anyone over the age of 14. They were hardly used in Blair's first term. But in the second term they became central to the Respect Agenda, along with the teaching of citizenship in schools. The orders saw youths banned from playing football, wearing gloves and, in their more comical form, sent a woman to prison for loud sex.

The real targets were the "yobs", the estate boys – those who had always made the gentry tremble. The orders were issued by the courts alongside parenting programmes. Those subject to the orders had their liberties severely restricted for a minimum of two years. Encouraged, the government began to deploy parenting orders, family intervention projects and dispersal orders, fundamentally restricting liberties, entitlements and rights on the basis of values and behaviour.

While Blair's Respect Agenda had echoes of past patrician attempts at civilizing the residuum, now it was the state itself that directly dispensed the lessons, proactively criminalizing the estate youth and dispensing punitive measures. Put another way, the social contract had been rewritten to make sure that responsibilities preceded rights. ASBOs were the muscular arm of the state, deployed to keep order whilst the harm from organized negligence began to stir tensions.

AUDACIOUS OUTSOURCING

The end of Tory rule left a society increasingly polarized between a property-owning class and renters who found it harder and harder to secure a decent home and living standard. What, for a century, had been called "council housing" now went through a linguistic shift that revealed the state's immediate removal: by the early 1990s, housing associations became virtually the only bodies able to build "social housing". As should have become clear by now, Thatcher's pursuit of a property-owning democracy was completed by New Labour. Blair and Brown accepted and propelled the inflation of house prices to drive the boom years they rode. In many ways, organized negligence was a strategy mainstreamed by New Labour.

In 2000, Labour introduced its Decent Homes Standard, which enabled a programme of investment that promised to bring the social housing rental sector into the twenty-first century. As a condition of accessing the funds, councils had to make serious decisions about their stock. One route lay in selling specific estates or their entire portfolio to housing associations, which were now classified as registered social landlords. Alternatively, councils could transfer their housing assets to an ALMO, which would manage the stock commercially with a corporate structure on behalf of the council. Councils could also enter into a public finance initiative or PFI. Although begun under John Major's tenure, PFIs were the bedrock of New Labour's Third Way, essentially allowing lucrative profits to be generated in the short-term meeting of social needs. Ultimately, though, the fees included in these arrangements compromised the long-term provision of services.

All these choices produced the same tension. On the one hand, a decision to keep housing stock owned and managed by the council came with financial straightjackets, leading to a cliff edge when it came to funding. On the other hand, stock transfers were resisted by tenants and Labour councillors across the country, who saw in them an inevitable raising of rents and increasingly precarious tenancies.

Case in point, Kensington and Chelsea Tenant Management Organisation (KCTMO), the largest tenant management organization in the country with a portfolio that included Grenfell Tower. In theory, the new structures ensured tenant voice by electing residents to the company board. However, in the KCTMO such representation was nominal and tokenistic. A once overbearing council was replaced by outsourced contractors. The issues remained, though many residents felt gaslighted by the processes. Contractors never seemed to be fully briefed on the issues reported, and often lacked the tools to complete their repair work. At the time of the Grenfell fire, the KCTMO had a backlog of 3,500 repairs (Barker 2018).

The Decent Homes initiative resulted in a million homes sold off to housing associations and another million homes managed by ALMOs and PFI vehicles. Over the 13 years of New Labour, less council housing was built than in Thatcher's final year in office (Hodkinson & Robbins 2013). Although access to low-interest loans kept the social housing sector buoyant, repairs and renovations suffered. Private sector actors often tended bids that undercut the other at the expense of public safety and standards. The squalor so many suffer today is due in good part to this underbelly of social housing. Above all, PFIs and ALMOs tended to remove the direct accountability of any publicly funded body to regulate their industries.

There is a sense of being muted which comes with organized negligence. As Daniel Hewitt's award-winning journalism of late has brought to light, thousands of people are living in homes unfit for human habitation – houses where the walls and ceilings cascade with toxic water, and where the mould contaminates every material. Even when residents complain about the conditions in front of their eyes they are informed that "there is no leak".

Such state-led policy has led to the UK public sector operating the second largest outsourcing market, after the United States. This, too, is an element of state negligence. Duties to house adequately, which exist in theory, cannot be properly represented in budgets. But this is not just an issue for those on social housing.

For private renters, conditions have also significantly worsened. The market is now saturated with agents taking exorbitant fees while landlords remain at arm's length.

Once upon a time, combustible products were outright banned in the UK. There was also a time when municipal authorities were responsible for building controls and had to ensure that buildings granted planning permission were in accordance with regulations. Nowadays these roles are outsourced and duty has been replaced with a profit incentive. Consider, especially, fire prevention. In March 1997 the Building Research Establishment was privatized. Building control became "an industry" to quote Brian Martin – a supposed fire safety expert, despite only having a diploma in building control surveying. When asked at the Grenfell Tower Inquiry whether he had any fire safety experience, he replied "I would have installed some fire doors" (Apps 2022).

Martin's testimony at the inquiry demonstrates that competition in the field has led to a reduction in standards. In the building control market, keeping the contract and maintaining a good relationship has usually prompted controllers to assist industry in reaching compliance. Since Tony Blair stood up his Better Regulation Task Force in 2005, building regulations have either been cut, or enforcements has been neutralized by market incentives. It is here that outsourcing – and the distribution and fragmentation of responsibilities – intersects with deregulation.

DANGEROUS DEREGULATION

During the Thatcher government Britain started to move towards a "performance based" system of fire prevention, as opposed to a prescriptive system, which would ban dangerous materials outright. A focus on performance shifts the rubric of compliance to the behaviour of any particular building in the event of a fire. Industry itself determines what a safe building is and the materials it can use, with little to no regulatory oversight of this determination.

To avoid liability for a catastrophic failure, developers follow the guidance of the government – in this case, Approved Document B. If the developer meets the performance-based standards, there is a presumption they are not liable for breaching regulations.

The ramifications of deregulation – whether formal or informal – are demonstrated in the Lakanal House fire. As part of a major refurbishment of the Sceaux Gardens Estate in Camberwell South London, the tower of Lakanal House was slated to be demolished. In the end, though, the authorities decided upon a £3.5 million refurbishment of the high-rise, undertaken between 2006 and 2007. High pressure laminate (HPL) cladding was fitted to the exterior of the building. Made by compressing wood and resin, the cladding was combustible.

On 3 July 2009 a fire broke out in flat 65. The occupant of the residence along with five others died. Catherine Hickman, a fashion designer, was on the phone to emergency services for 40 minutes before she perished. Clearly distressed, Hickman told the emergency operator that she could not breathe as she coughed and choked on smoke. She was urged to remain in her flat. The theory of compartmentation overrode reason. Even as flames lapped at her door, she was told to stay put, which she did as the ceiling began to collapse around her. She eventually fell silent, still on the line. The fire at Lakanal House moved quickly and unpredictably.

The coroner's report called for a review of Building Regulations. The problem in the government's existing documents was a fundamental ambiguity as to what was the standard of safety. It was not clear whether limited combustibility was sufficient, which would require materials to "survive in a 750°C furnace for two hours", or whether materials had to meet Class 0 – a standard far easier to pass and which would require a surface to resist the spread of flame even if behind that surface lay highly flammable materials. Insulation was held to a higher standard, although industry worked on the bad faith that cladding materials would never separate in the event of a fire, thereby exposing flammable insulation.

The fundamental ambiguity of standards could have been addressed in 2000 as part of a harmonization with EU regulations and standards. However, the Labour government was warned by the consultancy firm Warrington Fire that such a move "would severely restrict the market choice in terms of materials for specifiers and clients". So the government opted instead to maintain a regulatory ambiguity which meant that products banned in parts of Europe could be fitted in high-rises, even after they had caused death (Apps 2022).

At the time of writing, as of February 2022, materials can be used on high-rise buildings even if they are not of limited combustibility so long as they are Class 0 or pass a large-scale test from the Building Research Establishment (BRE). The test was supposed to be mandatory after several fires in the late 1990s, but this was never enacted. A system passes the BRE test if fire does not reach the top of the structure within 30 minutes and temperatures do not exceed 600°C.

Each test costs manufacturers £15,000. The tests are highly secretive and if a company's product fails, the details of its failure are very hard to discover. Additionally, it is the company, not the BRE, that sets up the test, which allows for creative mechanisms – such as introducing barriers or changing formulas – to be introduced so as to pass and reach compliance. In any case, materials that have been passed individually can be combined based only on a "desktop study".

Thus, in the absence of any coherent review of regulations, the government has effectively allowed industry to build with petrol. Even when risks were known, senior figures minimized them in order to avoid "market distortion" to quote Brian Martin again. But as the Grenfell Inquiry team reminded him, the "distortion" is merely pointing out that some materials are more flammable or combustible than others. Indeed, Martin even assured government that the risk of an ACM cladding fire was minimal in the UK, even though that was the exact type that burned Grenfell Tower (Stein 2022). New trends in home modernization have now spread this danger across the nation's housing stock.

Many recent regenerations of tower blocks have been led by concerns over carbon emissions and energy efficiency. While attending to security issues, these regenerations have also been designed to change the brutalist aesthetics of blocks, so disparaged by Prince Charles. Of course, relabelling a "tower block" an "apartment complex" is part of gentrification. Effectively, such renaming signals that the building is now populated by the deserving, upwardly mobile young professional class rather than the criminal, dysgenic underclass with its "problem families". Hence, due to the pervasiveness of outsourcing and deregulation, many buildings once considered squalid now present as defensible, private residential abodes.

Increasingly, however, these presentations and assumptions hide a disturbing reality. Leveraged up to the hilt with mortgage and other household debt, leaseholders seeking to join the property ladder now live with the dreadful uncertainty of a fate approximating those who lived at Grenfell Tower. Organized negligence might take root in the locales popularly associated with squalor, but its branches have now spread far and wide.

9

Twenty-first century squalor

As the 2008 financial crisis spread across the global economy, the Labour government intervened to prop up the housing market by supporting mortgage lenders and offering tax concessions to those purchasing homes. Despite many commentators accrediting Labour with "saving the system", the 2010 election resulted in a Conservative and Liberal Democrat coalition government, who promptly made it their priority to tighten the proverbial belt.

British people, the new government claimed, had "lived beyond their means". Chancellor George Osborne announced that it was time to "cut the waste and reform the welfare system that our country can no longer afford". As part of this austerity agenda, Osborne and Prime Minister David Cameron confronted a housing benefit bill that had mushroomed from £2 billion in the early 2000s to £20 billion in 2010. Logically, they sought to cut expenditure on the four million council and housing association homes where almost a fifth of the population still lived.

At the same time, lobbyists and Conservative politicians claimed that the Labour government had stifled the housing market by subsidizing council and social homes. Incredible as it might seem, Conservative ideologues judged the deregulation and outsourcing of the Blair years to have been insufficient to the task of unleashing the full potential of that market. In short, the coalition government was dead set on turning Thatcher's property-owning democracy almost fully over into a landlord's oligarchy.

Recall the definition we gave to squalor at the start of this book: your habitat kills you. In the previous chapter we considered New Labour's strategy of public–private financing, deregulation and outsourcing to have led to an organized negligence practiced by the state and its local administrations. In this chapter, we track the logical endpoint of such a strategy, a form of what Cameroonian philosopher Achille Mbembe (2003) has called "necropolitics". For Mbembe, contemporary politics is defined not necessarily by a straightforward desire to kill populations, but by a right to expose particular populations to deadly conditions.

We argue that after 2010 the British state has effectively divided the population into those who cling to a category of "life" – people who comfortably own habitations that are constructed safely – and those deposited in a category of "death" – those occupying habitations that they can ill afford and are unsafe, as well as the homeless and asylum seekers. With regards to the former category, we identify a government push to privatize; and with regards to the latter category, we identify a push to criminalize. These two pushes have combined to provide the form and fluidity of twenty-first-century squalor.

THE PUSH TO PRIVATIZE

Despite proclamations of a "compassionate conservatism" while in opposition, the Conservative Party, in government again, enthusiastically embraced an ideas industry that promoted market-driven statecraft. To purify the state of its non-market pathologies required welfare to be not only shrunk but made even more conditional.

In 2010, the highly influential Conservative think tank, Policy Exchange, began publishing reports seeking to nudge the government into an assault on welfare. Their report, *Making Housing*

Affordable (Morton 2010), claimed that social housing was a "poverty trap". Utilizing a centuries old argument that state welfare bred dependency, they advocated that social housing be treated like private rentals yielding market rents. Their long-term vision was, effectively, to emulate 1930s Britain, when the private building sector met most housing needs in a huge economic boom. They also proposed cutting the red tape so that offices could be converted to housing.

The Localism Act of 2011 was one of the first creations of this new policy nexus. The Act scrapped lifelong tenancies in social housing, replacing them with two- or five-year tenancies, though discretion was shown by authorities and housing associations. The Housing Secretary Grant Shapps opined it was "no longer right to require each social tenancy be for life". The move did not prove to be universal, but its message was simple: housing was allocated on the basis of need and could be taken away on the same basis. Like all welfare, it was now granted conditionally.

Conditionality took a number of forms. Residents, for instance, lost the right to pass tenancies from parent to child. The cruelty of this policy is suggested by social media stories of evictions swiftly following the death of a parent. More cruelty: if social housing was to be allocated on the basis of need, then logic dictated that it could be taken away if tenants were no longer in need – that is, if they were deemed capable of paying private rents. Moreover, a cap was introduced which fully funded the cheapest third of homes but made tenants liable to paying anything more expensive. This policy owed far more to Beveridge than Bevan as it questioned why the taxpayer should fund those who live in *areas* beyond their means. Weekly household payments were capped at £400, regardless of household size. Such callous moves gave the lie to Beveridge's hopes that government would redress the "adequacy of provision" problem.

To put it bluntly, decentralization did not shift power from central to local government but, rather, from local government to private enterprise. Or, to put it in the words of Jessica Perera (2019), the Localism Act created "responsibility without power, local government without the power to govern". The act made local authorities increasingly dependent upon the revenue of big business and developments to find any budget, given the scale of government cuts in real terms. This was a straightforward inversion of 1970s municipalism.

If that was not enough, the Welfare Reform Act of 2012 introduced a new mechanism of adjudication, termed "social rented sector size criterion", or more popularly known as the "bedroom tax". Any tenant who was found to have a spare bedroom had this so-called "subsidy" removed. In practice, this resulted in a 14 per cent reduction of benefits for the existence of one spare bedroom, and a 25 per cent reduction for two spares.

The government claimed that the move was intended to cut the housing benefit bill and reduce overcrowding. Yet, quite simply, there was insufficient housing stock to downsize to. No surprise, then, that although the government estimated some 30 per cent of those affected by the policy would move as a consequence, only 6 per cent did; the rest became even poorer. Worries over debt, rent arrears and eviction produced a profound sense of hopelessness, with increased cases of anxiety and depression. Disabled residents who needed an extra room for their carer or medical equipment were still penalized.

Even more cuts and conditionality followed. The new Universal Credit scheme centralized benefits into one payment, further reducing their value. The scheme then paid Housing Benefit directly to tenant's bank accounts, many of whom were straddling multiple debts and commitments. In short, benefits were often eaten by debt. Already struggling, tenants fell into further arrears leading to hundreds of thousands of evictions from social housing. In the first half of the coalition government, the amount of people accepted as homeless by local authorities grew by 26 per cent, whereas street homelessness grew by 37 per cent. Over this period, homeless households forced to shelter in temporary accommodation grew by 14 per cent (Tunstall 2015).

With benefit caps in place, London and other big cities became too expensive for the poorest to live in. So, many were moved by their local councils to where the cost of living was cheaper but where their social security networks were non-existent. This was a process of decanting not unfamiliar to early-twentieth-century policies. But the causal link between a demand for housing and the inflating cost of rent and housing was not taken seriously by the government, nor the price of land.

In a bid to "get Britain building", the coalition fundamentally changed planning legislation through the creation of the National Planning Policy Framework (NPPF) in 2012. The changes were designed to make planning permission easier to obtain with a "general presumption in favour of development". Policy Exchange proposed burning regulatory red tape so that offices could be converted to housing. "Our current planning system", opined Alex Morton, "designed as part of a socialist utopia in the 1940s, has to be modernized for a 21st-century economy". Nick Boles, who had formed the think tank, became Minister of Planning and in 2013 sanctioned the conversion projects.

Local authorities hold little to no control over such developments, a problem amplified by the fact that developers of these projects have been able to avoid architectural norms. Although Britain still had restrictions on the height of tenements and blocks of flats, office blocks could be nonetheless built much higher. Office blocks did not require the same kinds of compartmentalization as residential blocks. Less fire-proof materials could thus be used. And whereas residential blocks operate a "stay put" policy, office blocks have periodic evacuation drills. Suffice to say, no office block conversion should have a stay put policy. The point is that blocks are designed differently for work as opposed to habitation.

In 2018, Terminus House – an office block and the tallest

structure in the New Town of Harlow – was converted to residential. It has come to shelter the most vulnerable in society,
from single mothers to recent releases from prison. The rooms
are tiny and lack natural light. The building is fitted with over
100 high-resolution CCTV cameras and is policed digitally. Paul
Jackson, the regional manager at Caridon Property who owns and
runs Terminus, has dubbed the property a "stepping stone" for
people of "lower income". In Harlow, Terminus House has become
synonymous with crime; police district commander chief inspector Matt Cornish is "convinced" that the block breeds anti-social
behaviour (Precey, Sturdy & Cawley 2019).

Consider, too, that Terminus House was converted less than
one year after the Grenfell Tower fire. No policy has since been
reversed. Over half the new housing for Harlow will be office conversions, where people eat, drink and sleep in their beds. We might
therefore consider Terminus House to be a hallmark of twenty-
first-century squalor, housing those cleared from the city's more
expensive areas, building up density in towns now stripped of
industry, and maintaining order with high-resolution cameras.

However, it was not just Conservatives who pushed to privatize the housing sector and conditionalize public provision. In 2015
the Labour peer, Andrew Adonis, released a report entitled *City
Villages* which called for postwar estates to be designated "brownfield sites", which in planning terms means post-industrial.
Adonis complained that, when it came to inner cities, most land
was owned by local authorities and remained significantly under-
developed since the 1970s. He proposed to create "city villages" on
these sites. Subsequently, Adonis was appointed by the Conservative government to chair an independent National Infrastructure
Commission.

In 2016 the Conservative government legislated a Housing and Planning Act. Planning permission was now granted
in principle to any housing development on sites featured in a
statutory register of brownfield land, which now included many

already-populated council housing estates. It was proposed that local authorities would be obliged to sell properties deemed high value once they became vacant, although this did not ultimately come into force.

Where redevelopments have taken place, large estates are decanted in sections alongside phased demolitions and rebuilds. Often this process takes between five and ten years. Moss Side's recent redevelopments are a case in point: rows of empty houses have been left, leaving residents at risk. By classifying housing estates as brownfield, their residents, mostly working class, are imagined as "industrial waste" – a twenty-first-century residuum (Elmer & Dening 2016).

Amidst this detritus, Britain's biggest developers have been busy land-banking rather than fulfilling need. Land-banking pertains to the practice of holding land to maximize value via maintaining the scarcity of homes, which inflates house prices. Even in 2007 the Callcutt Review acknowledged that Britain's big builders are "identifying, acquiring, preparing, developing and selling land" which is now a "key activity of all [UK] house building companies". A recent House of Lords (2016) report claims that in 2015, Persimmon, Taylor Wimpey and Barratt had planning permission for 200,000 homes, yet only built 44,000. Combined, their "strategic land holdings" far outstrip their land which enjoys permission to build. Liam Halligan (2019) estimates that these strategic holdings could yield some 500,000 more homes.

Yet the process of land-banking goes way beyond builders and developers. In 2012, it was estimated that 45 per cent of residential planning applications granted was on land owned by companies who had never built anything (Mayor of London 2014). The trading of land has therefore become a lucrative market unto itself, to the detriment of the vast majority of city dwellers. To be fair, this strategy is only a logical consequence of the Land Compensation Act of 1961 which, as we argued in Chapter 5, set in place the principle that betterment accrues principally to the developer and landowner rather than to the denizens of the city.

Market-driven statecraft has also encouraged private rentals. In their bid to get the economy back on track, the coalition government restricted housing supply significantly and doubled down on an increased dependency on property and land prices to facilitate GDP growth. This strategy, of course, required the housing sector to be increasingly financialized. The Department for Communities and Local Government's capital budget for new housing was cut 54 per cent during the coalition's time in power. Government grants to housing associations for new building was cut by two-thirds, leading to an increased reliance by the sector on private capital to fund projects.

More financialization led to higher rates of repayment and interest, which trickled down into higher rent payments for tenants. The high cost of rents prevents many from saving, let alone gathering enough money for a deposit. As the campaigning group Generation Rent has found, "the average couple in a private tenancy pays 41 per cent of their income on rent, compared to 18 per cent for home owners and 30 per cent for social tenants". The vast majority of landlords own their property on buy-to-let mortgage schemes. Landlords account for less than 2 per cent of the British population, but the power they now exert has become significant (Dorling 2015). Meanwhile, as the homeless charity Crisis suggests, the cost of rent has been one of the major causal factors in the proliferation of food banks, which now outnumber McDonalds branches in Britain.

Currently, the Conservative government aspire to turn "generation rent into generation buy", although their own economic policies make such a transformation impossible. As noted in Chapter 3, when the house-building boom of the 1930s was in full swing, the British population experienced a rise in living standards and disposable income. Not only that, but there was at least some general sense of an upward trajectory with rising wages.

In contrast, younger generations today feel themselves to be entirely priced out of the property market – even in their home cities. The number of private renters has more than doubled since 1997, with 5 million households currently in the sector. By 2050, on current trends, most British people will live in private rental accommodation.

Furthermore, it is estimated that at least 13 per cent of privately rented homes in England alone – some 619,000 houses – fail safety standards completely, in contrast to the social rented sector where the number is considered to be closer to 5 per cent (something still entirely unacceptable). A quarter of housing stock available is technically safe but in disrepair, with damp, cold or mould ubiquitous. In 2016, some 28 per cent of homes in the private rental sector failed to meet the government's own Decent Homes standard. Hence, when the coalition government scrapped Housing Market Renewal and significantly changed the finance of Decent Homes obligation, it set course for further deterioration of much of Britain's housing stock.

But might home owners really be more secure than private renters?

Post-financial crisis, the government stimulated the housing market with a "Help to Buy" programme (see Tunstall 2015). This was, in effect, a parody of the "Right to Buy" and principally offered cheaper loans to help buyers bid for over-priced houses they could not otherwise afford. (Incidentally, Homes England, the central government agency, outsourced the Help to Buy programme to Target, a private company.) The policy was widely criticized across the ideological spectrum in so far as it helped to inflate demand and maintain house prices at a level that increased generational divides. Most young adults were priced out, with only high-earning professionals able to qualify for the scheme.

Two-thirds of first-time buyers have since used the programme to place their feet on an increasingly precipitous first rung of the housing ladder. Oftentimes they have purchased apartments in medium-to-high-rise complexes. Not only have residents suffered from punitively high "ground rents" imposed under the long lease they are granted on the property. Additionally, deregulation has led to defective blocks. In such a permissive environment, a catalogue of fire safety issues, already prevalent under the regulations of New Labour's governance, have increased. Wooden balconies, untreated timber, a lack of fire barriers and other fire risks now affect a large proportion – if not the majority – of new-build medium-to-high blocks. And highly flammable cladding systems have been applied to both new builds and redevelopments.

When the Adam Smith Institute, a free-market think tank, framed Help to Buy as "throwing petrol onto a bonfire" they were talking about the crisis of affordability. We now know that this was not simply a metaphor. If squalor, simply defined, refers to a habitat that kills, then we might say that it is principally in the private sector where this giant now lurks.

THE PUSH TO CRIMINALIZE

Tony Blair introduced New Labour as a project that would save those forgotten by Thatcher. Before long, that salvation was provided through a series of incredibly punitive policies. Similarly, the "compassionate conservatism" of David Cameron came with a focus on "nudging" rather than compulsion. Nudge theory is a concept in behavioural economics, proposing that indirect influences can be used to impact the behaviours of groups or individuals (Sunstein & Thaler 2014). Once again, though, and especially when it came to the residents of estates, nudging quickly turned into callous compulsion.

One year into the coalition government and a series of England's cities exploded in riots and uprisings. The proximate cause was the execution by police of Mark Duggan, a resident of Broadwater Farm estate in Tottenham. In the immediate aftermath, locals sought answers. The Duggan family were not informed by police of his killing until a day and half after he was killed. A march on 6 August was organized from Broadwater Farm to Tottenham police station. Duggan's family wanted an explanation of what had happened. The Met did not send out one senior officer to address those congregated. When police broke up the demonstration, treating a female protester in a heavy-handed manner, the demonstration turned riotous.

Tottenham burned. At first, the events were local but then spread to other London boroughs. For the first two-to-three nights, events remained within London. Then the disorder broke out in the Midlands and cities across the north of England. By the end, some 66 riots and uprisings had broken out across the country and 2,500 commercial properties were destroyed. Five people lost their lives in the violent unrest.

We contend that the riots and uprisings must be placed in the same context as the struggles for the city we recounted in Chapter 6. We use both terms – riots *and* uprisings – because not all the unrest was politically motivated in an intentional sense, and certainly, there was plenty of opportunism on display. Nevertheless, as a general phenomenon, the 2011 disturbances could be considered a response by youth to their virtual incarceration and devaluation by decades of housing policies that resulted in an organized neglect of their neighbourhoods.

Meanwhile, invocations of the residuum – of "underclasses" and "problem families" – abounded amongst the political and chattering classes as if the Dickensian era had never finished. Well-to-do sojourners adventurously roamed the hidden dens and colonies of the inner city seeking out a "caste apart". A narrative, in particular, of "broken Britain" reached feverish levels as reporters attempted to deduce reason from such "wanton destruction" of the urban landscape (Hancock & Mooney 2013). Prime Minister David Cameron simplified the whole affair as "just pure criminality". Most importantly, he denied any relationship between the riots and austerity because, he reasoned, people looted shops rather than burned down Parliament.

We do not romanticize such actions. However, we do want to draw attention to the partiality of judgement, because these actions were cast as an abomination to the true – orderly – working class. Rather than corporate raiders or risk-bearing entrepreneurs, these enterprising youth were described by Conservative Justice Secretary Kenneth Clarke as "a feral underclass, cut off from the mainstream in everything but its materialism" (Lewis, Taylor & Ball 2011). Clarke drew upon the discourse of problem families to pathologize their actions and to suggest that nudging would not work on this animalized residue of humanity – those "individuals and families familiar with the justice system, who haven't been changed by their past punishments". Clarke's prescription was to reform the criminal justice system so as to forcibly inculcate values that would prevent destructive "anti-social" behaviour.

One might ask: absent a commitment to provide general needs, and given the draining, outsourcing and deregulation of social housing, what is there left for government to govern save for a moral crisis? As we have shown, moral crises over squalor have always proceeded through a distinction between those dysgenic to and those fit-to-compete over capital accumulation. "Feral" is but a twenty-first-century update to the "residuum". As Lucy Easthope, one of Britain's leading disaster planners, suggested to us, the word is used to dehumanize populations whom the state seeks to discipline.

In the aftermath of the riots, the cuts that had already been planned were enacted through a series of legislative changes that fundamentally challenged the urban youth's right to the city. In fact, similar to Thatcher's use of the moral crisis over muggers, Cameron deployed the menace of violent estate youth to justify the welfare reforms described above. He explicitly made the argument that the full force of new sanctions could be wielded against those guilty of rioting, suggesting, for example, that households of convicted individuals might be evicted. Indeed, such a measure was enacted by at least some local authorities and housing associations. This was nothing less than collective punishment.

Government subsequently overhauled antisocial behaviour orders. Injunctions to prevent nuisance and annoyance (IPNA) were introduced as part of the Anti-Social Behaviour, Crime and Policing Act of 2014. The new powers allowed the state to prosecute, fine or even imprison anyone over the age of ten. What is more, IPNAs could now be issued by housing providers, which effectively gave councils and housing associations legal jurisdiction over their tenants.

No surprise, then, that as local services were cut to near oblivion, some of the youth began to do the same. Levels of youth violence grew considerably, particularly knife crime. A fear of urban environments grew resurgent, with many right-wing commentators depicting the major cities as being overrun by violent hordes. In response, the government pledged "a concerted all-out war on gangs and gang culture".

These references to war should not be taken casually. At various points in this book, we have noted how the reproduction of squalor rests upon not just a class division but a race/class distinction that consistently threatens to treat dysgenic populations as a "caste apart" – a disease that must be suppressed or expunged from the body politic. The thin line that separates policing from warfare rests on a precarious and mobile distinction between citizens and non-citizens. Collective punishment, for instance, is outlawed by the Geneva convention.

It is with this in mind that we turn to the "gang matrix" developed by the Metropolitan police in the aftermath of 2011. The same logics that defined Broadwater Farm as a criminal estate were at play in the matrix. The new policing model targeted young adults out of education and training who were deemed "at risk" of future uprisings. In the database's profile of criminal groupings in

London, three quarters were of African-Caribbean backgrounds, with approximately 85 per cent categorized as Black, Asian and Minority Ethnic. Veteran Tottenham rights campaigner Stafford Scott has called the database "inherently and intrinsically" racist.

Chillingly, in the London borough of Haringey, which includes Tottenham, 42 per cent of residents initially included in the matrix had no recorded history of involvement in violence. Moreover, police regularly share information on youth in the database with local authorities and housing associations who then consider these individuals "risky" even in the absence of evidence. The wellbeing and security of an individual's whole household are at stake in this information sharing. According to one staff member of a Borough Gangs Unit, eviction threats were one of the "three most celebrated tactics" used by police, along with imprisonment and deportation (Amnesty International UK Section 2018).

We would argue that the intensification of policing and counter-terrorism instruments now runs parallel and seeks to discipline estate residents whose communalism hides them from proper state surveillance. This parallelism might even be of signal importance to understanding twenty-first-century squalor.

A National Domestic Extremism Database was formed in 2004 and fully digitalized. The information is highly secretive and is protected by the intelligence wing of the Metropolitan Police, the National Special Branch Intelligence System (NSBIS). The database is allegedly extensive, including known domestic extremists and anyone they associate with. Operations are managed within existing regional Counter Terrorism Unit structures.

Meanwhile, in the two decades since the dawn of the "war on terror", some nine Acts of Parliament have been passed, legitimizing sweeping powers of the state and authorities including mass surveillance. Central to the battle against terrorism is the government's Prevent agenda, a form of total surveillance based on an early-warning system that is supposed to track "radicalization". Particular areas have become associated with Islamic radicalism, with a heat map showing the most "at risk". In some areas, there has been overlap between counter-terrorism and operations like Trident – the Met police-led operation against Black violence.

Increasingly, then, one might say that lines have been blurred. The attitude to public order, much like terrorism, is to prevent. So, mass surveillance has been sanctioned, including not only political activists as such, but also disaffected youth and young adults. In fact, the coalition government brought a set of offices together to form the National Domestic Extremism Unit (NDEU), which was further reformed into the National Domestic Extremism and Disorder Intelligence Unit. Note the concatenation of extremism and disorder. We would therefore argue that it is increasingly difficult to separate criminalization from de-citizen-ization. This blurring of punishment, exclusion and civic excommunication would not be possible save for the push to privatize one of the most basic needs of humanity – shelter.

MARKET FANTASIES

Riffing off Stuart Hall, political economist Ian Bruff (2014) has labelled the era of austerity "authoritarian neoliberalism". Of course, one of the ethical principles underlying neoliberalism has always been the claim that states are not only inefficient at allocating resources but unjust in the process – placing constraints on the ability of individuals to determine their own interests. Yet as we have documented, the effects of neoliberalism have been anything but freeing for residents of maligned estates. At the start of this chapter we suggested that the contemporary state follows two distinct but parallel principles: a right to life, via privatization, and an allowance of death, via criminalization.

Such a logical contradiction between freedom and unfreedom, life and death, can only be sustained by considering the market – and its ability to impartially adjudicate and supply needs – in fantastical terms. We would submit that a necessary and foundational element of such fantasy is the stubborn depiction of estate residents as squalid.

After 2011, Cameron unleashed a politics of development and redevelopment, which responded to polling that suggested huge support for stripping tenancies from rioters. Repeating the deeply engrained assumption that "terraced streets or low-rise apartment buildings" were not environments that bred crime and disorder, Cameron contended that the "rioters came overwhelmingly from these postwar estates". Summoning the argument of Newman's *Defensible Space*, Cameron decried the "brutal high-rise towers and dark alleyways" where the criminals dwelt and the drug dealers plied their wares (*Sunday Times* 2016). Cameron targeted Broadwater Farm explicitly. Yet since its £33 million redevelopment, the estate had enjoyed lower crime rates than most of London and the lowest rate of rent arrears in Haringey. (The area was also primed for redevelopment through a contentious land development vehicle.)

In another report, *Create Streets* (2013), Policy Exchange (again) suggested the demolition of all London high-rises, amounting to 360,000 council homes. Replacing them would be a traditional low-rise street plan. Private owners would live next to residents taking advantage of "affordable housing", to enjoy well-lit, surveilled and highly-sanitized neighbourhoods replete with "village developments". A website was setup to further promote the vision to "build London along better lines both to improve lives and help solve our housing crisis". Savills, the real estate company, added their weight to the argument, with their own report *Completing London's Streets*, which called for mass demolition and regeneration as a means of raising house prices across the city.

What the policy advisers seemed to miss was twofold. Firstly, the Bevanite principle of general needs was predicated, precisely, on a desire to create mixed communities (Boughton 2018). Alternatively, the residualization of the social housing sector has been the outcome of housing policies pushed by Conservative politicians from Harold Macmillan onwards. Secondly, through the Right to Buy programme, many estates have actually become mixed communities, with private professionals occupying flats and council homes. Nevertheless, a mono-classist fantastical image of estates and their dwellers has enabled an easy moralistic distinction to obtain that, just as it had for Charles Booth, conflates residents with their surroundings with their distance from God. No tower block suffered more under this fantastical – and almost theological – distinction than Grenfell Tower.

10

Social murder

In this concluding chapter, we return once more to North Kensington, London. It should have become clear by now that many of the historical, political and theoretical threads of this book lead to the fire at Grenfell Tower, in the Lancaster West Estate. In the Introduction, we claimed that squalor is inextricably bound to mortality and an ever-increasing proximity to death. The Grenfell Tower fire, we suggest, is the form that twenty-first-century squalor takes – and might take again. Those who consider themselves far removed from the stereotypical figure of squalor – criminal, impoverished, living off benefits and in broken social housing – might now need to reassess their proximities.

FIGHTING FIRE

With an unprecedented swing in the 2017 snap election, Labour candidate Emma Dent Coad took London's Kensington constituency. Dent Coad's incredibly close victory was cheered on by participants of several local movements campaigning for public space under the Westway, for the retention of local amenities, and for housing justice in general. Amongst the crowd gathered outside the Town Hall was Ed Daffarn of the Grenfell Action Group who was busy encouraging electoral observers to investigate the local council. With Dent Coad's victory the press began to pay attention to this working-class community in the heart of London, which, despite waves of gentrification, remained embedded in the wards of North Kensington.

Days later, Ed Daffarn barely survived Britain's deadliest residential fire since the Blitz. The scale of the crime has now become clear to all, with the Grenfell Tower Inquiry revealing a widespread knowledge of the risks of the cladding system and insulation. Arconic, Celotex and Kingspan were well aware of the combustibility of their products, but they still marketed them as safe.

As we have noted, the government as well as privatized regulatory bodies knew that the products sold by corporate crooks and killers presented a significant threat to life. They allowed the ambiguous classification of Class 0 to hold for products they knew to be combustible, because they did not want to "distort the market" by specifying what was safe or unsafe. Deceiving themselves wilfully, they did not even plan for the eventuality of serious cladding fire, despite evidence from a number of domestic and international incidents.

London accounts for more high-rises than the rest of the country combined; the Borough of Westminster alone has almost as many as the city of Manchester. Yet at the time, the London fire service possessed no adequate ladders for fighting a high-rise fire. The only equipment high enough to fight Grenfell Tower's flames was in Surrey, at the Thorpe Park theme park. Clearly, on 14 June 2017, the fire brigade was not prepared to evacuate Grenfell Tower and simply could not fight the fire.

However, long before the fire took hold, the redevelopment of the tower block had been a constant source of misery for the residents. The Grenfell Action Group (GAG) was founded when the project to build an academy school (the Kensington and Aldridge Academy) and a leisure centre on public space and land commenced. This was of particular importance to residents of Grenfell as they did not have balconies, yet the proposed development would have destroyed the public space next to Grenfell

Tower which included a playground, a public green, and sports pitches.

In 2009, the Royal Borough of Kensington and Chelsea (RBKC) commissioned Urban Initiatives to redevelop the historic area of Notting Dale (now referred to as Notting Barns, but locally dubbed "Latimer" due to its proximity to Latimer Road Tube station). The company's executive summary included an intention to demolish most of the housing in the area, including Grenfell Tower. The houses built to mark the end of the slums, in a historic working-class neighbourhood, would disappear. In their place would stand new builds, 60 per cent affordable and 40 per cent private housing, a "significant" amount of which would comprise "terraced houses and ground floor maisonettes with direct access to the street".

As we have noted many times, bucolic fantasies of low-rise living replacing high-rise slums rarely seem to include the continued presence of existing residents. Indeed, with no provision of social housing per se, the redevelopment threatened to price out many local residents. The local authority's decant policy provided no right to return for residents moved out of the borough. And so Grenfell activists fought from the outset against the plans. It is their belief that it was only austerity measures and local government cuts that led to the redevelopment taking on a less radical form. Instead, £10 million was allocated to Grenfell Tower for cladding that would fit the aesthetic of the new leisure centre and school.

As the residents of Grenfell began to question the redevelopment, their concerns were ignored by the authorities. Ed Daffarn told the public inquiry that he was "stigmatised as a troublemaker" for raising his voice against the KCTMO and local council. Daffarn described the expectation, from administrators and contracted firms, that residents should "be thankful for their service; or effectively be damned" (Daffarn 2020). For example, Daffarn remembers a Rydon employee informing him "I wouldn't mind if I were getting it for free". Contempt, it seems was also outsourced.

Because residents were blocked from forming an association, they organized by necessity outside of official channels. At various points in this book, we have proposed a subtle but important difference between a sense of "community" rendered transparent to government and abiding by its logics of order, and a practice of "communalism", opaque to government, sometimes jagged, possibly even self-destructive, but nonetheless driven fundamentally by a desire for justice and self-determination.

The GAG blog is an archive par excellence of this communalism, detailing over many years the concerns and arguments of residents. Astoundingly, the blog was blocked on the servers of KCTMO with staff and local councillors considering it a "source of disinformation" (Booth 2021). Although some of the posts could strike a comical or caustic tone, the quality of the work speaks for itself. Take, for instance, one post entitled "the Stairs of shame and other abuses..." wherein activists write: "If Grenfell Tower and the wider Lancaster West Estate was a child then it would have been taken into care by the Local Authority a long time ago for the abuses that it has received from those with responsibility for its well-being". Even before the fire, the British Library approached the authors and began the process of archiving the blog for posterity.

The Grenfell Action Group, Leaseholders Association and Grenfell Compact all raised serious concerns about fire safety risks in an articulate manner. After a cladding-related fire broke out a mile away from the tower at Shepherd's Court in 2016, the Grenfell Tower Leaseholder's Association contacted KCTMO and RBKC, requesting a fire drill. Ed Daffarn questioned the prevailing "stay put" policy: "I had always thought about if there was a gas explosion or something quite catastrophic happening and there was a need to get people out of the building in a quick way", he told the inquiry.

Crucially, a freedom of information request was made, regarding changes to the specifications of the refurbishment. It was denied. For if the residents had been furnished with this information, their due diligence would have revealed the severe risk that the council, KCTMO and contractors had put them under. So would have the independent review that they demanded. Instead, resident voices were muted. Blocked on servers. Cancelled in the most violent form, in a manner that goes back to the Victorian age.

Barbara Lane, an expert fire assessor who appeared at the inquiry, spoke of a "culture of non-compliance" that accompanied the management of the building and procurement of materials and services. Using the terminology that we have introduced in this book it might be said that KCTMO and RBKC partook of organized negligence, enabled at a structural level by deregulation and outsourcing. In fact, they neglected so comprehensively that the fire, when it came, was unique, being the first in the world to spread up, around and down.

There was not a part of Grenfell left unclad, not even its "architectural crown", a quirk of the building that designers decided to bend cladding cassettes to fit. Because of this detail, the fire was able to spread in ways that confounded the fire officers. Their seniors had been warned of such dangers, but the risks were never disseminated to the rank and file. There had been no training for such an eventuality. The training that they all relied on was "stay put". In the toxic environment of deregulation, it was a policy of organized negligence.

The vexatious complainers were right. One need only examine the current form of the KCTMO for proof: a shell, maintained purely for legal purposes. The Grenfell Tower Public Inquiry has revealed that the organization had a backlog of thousands of safety issues, including fire safety warnings and enforcement orders that were not acted upon. Amongst them were self-closing doors that did not function. The organization's failure to replace them and the widespread use of non-compliant fire doors was causative of the spread of smoke, responsible for the vast majority of deaths on the 14 June 2017.

A catalogue of failings from a vast array of institutions led to the loss of life at Grenfell. Despite the fire being out of control and out of reach, fire commanders maintained the assumption that the fire had not penetrated flats. It had. A police helicopter hovered above the tower, but the feed was not shared with the fire service. At 1.26am, the police declared a major incident with the expectation of significant loss of life, some 40 minutes before the fire service did.

Grenfell was a very real challenge to public order. As we have noted in previous chapters, there is always a political element to riots and civil unrest. The tacit acceptance of this element is what constitutes the kernel of one-nation Conservatism, anaemically revived by Theresa May during her short prime ministership. The will to slay the giant of squalor derived from the will to control the poor and their potentially radical politics. Recall Prime Minister Lloyd George admitting that building costs were a small price to pay to prevent Bolshevism. Almost 100 years after the first council housing Grenfell Tower burned in part, at least, because the political will to afford those costs had dissipated.

Grenfell was called a failure of state by Theresa May as she addressed parliament in the wake of the disaster. By the logic of social contract theory, when the state fails, the natural right to life trumps the laws of the state. And when the state threatens your life, you may take up arms against it, literally or metaphorically. The failures at Grenfell were severe enough to challenge the covenant many have with the state, which tacitly or expressly consents to the power invested in institutions – institutions that failed so catastrophically.

In the previous chapter we suggested that since 2011 fears of disorder have increasingly run parallel to fears over domestic terrorism. What brings both fears into relation is their locatedness

– in areas of squalor. Indeed, the fear of revolt loomed large in police operations that followed the Grenfell Tower fire. Lucy East-hope, at the time the Cabinet Lead for Disaster Recovery, relayed to us that police briefings warned of "another Duggan". The gov-ernment ran the operation along Prevent lines, using anti-terror mechanisms and social control operations. Armed response units patrolled the streets as residents searched for their loved ones.

The public order operation in the wake of the fire was vast, and much of it remains shrouded in secrecy. Speculation and conjecture aside, it seems that at least part of the strategy was to regain order through a selective control of information, a certain economical use of disinformation, and a disrupting of the com-munity's ability to organize meaningful responses. Compounding these difficulties was aid from well-wishers, which flooded the area, causing community organizers to focus principally on logistical efforts even though various attempts were made to com-municate that there existed a surfeit. The vast majority was not delivered to those in need, but it did fill community spaces for the summer. With the aid also came faith leaders, celebrities, and a variety of interlopers. Although many of them arrived in good faith, most painted the fire as a tragedy and not the crime that residential organizations knew it to be.

David Lammy, Labour MP for Tottenham, blamed the fire on "Corbusier-inspired" tower blocks, a logic that he had used a few years previously to explain the uprisings that followed the killing of Mark Duggan. Lammy spoke of the postwar estates as "criminally unsafe", where "families live in hutches, not houses" (Lammy 2017). His words were echoed by Policy Exchange, which called for "sincere negotiation away from the heat of politics" to achieve the aims of pulling down the postwar estates. A narrative quickly took hold in the media of Grenfell Tower as a twenty-first-century rookery full of illicit activity run by immi-grants, Muslims, Blacks, and the underclass. As Ben Okri put it, "If you want to see how the poor die, come see Grenfell Tower" (Okri

2017). But limiting Grenfell's scope to the poor entirely under-plays the scale of modern-day squalor.

Lammy rightfully called the fire a crime for which there must be arrests. Yet even here, he failed to grasp the nettle that Grenfell Tower was a victim of the new, not the old. This was London Mayor Sadiq Khan's misapprehension too: "we would not dream of building towers to the standards of the 1970s, but their inhabitants still have to live with that legacy" (Khan 2017). In fact, Grenfell had a solid record of fire safety before the redevelopment. In this particular case, it was not a 1970s standard that was to blame but rather a post-1980s deregulating and outsourcing of safety standards.

Grenfell Tower was not overcrowded. The undocumented population of London were held to have filled the tower, so people inflated the death toll into the hundreds and distorted any image of the tower block as it was. What is more, postcode data reveals that at the time of the fire, the resident population was, if relatively deprived, nonetheless upwardly aspirational in terms of education and skills-training. A minority were unemployed, with the majority either retired, carers, studying or working. Those who died were truly a cross-section of the locality, from aspiring sportsmen, to young mothers to artists. To quote the rapper Lowkey, they were the backbones and lungs of London.

Despite this census data, easily available, newspapers, broadcast news, journal articles and documentaries painted the area with "criminal classes" and undocumented migrants (dubbed "illegal" by the nativist press and political climate) – a black site on Charles Booth's map. In his final lines to the inquiry at his day of testimony, Ed Daffarn spoke of the "terrible things" said of the community after the fire. Such commentary hurt the community and deprived them of the opportunity to show what the community was like: "That thought is truly heart-breaking."

TO SLAY SQUALOR

At the beginning of this book, we laid out some questions for which we sought to provide illumination. What elements of squalor persist over time, even if squalor has changed its form? How might we name squalor in the present day? And what social forces might be committed to killing the giant? In conclusion, we will gesture towards some answers that arise out of our investigation of the Grenfell Tower fire.

In the wake of Grenfell, the cladding on social housing has been remediated at a far quicker rate than on private residential properties. In contrast, private leaseholders who have found their blocks covered in ACM cladding have faced the daily threat of death and financial misery for five years, with the government taking four and half years before promising to make the developers and building owners pay. Those who suffer from other fire defects, including the HPL cladding found on Lakanal House remain in incredibly precarious living conditions. Further deregulations have been announced since the fire, and relaxed planning conditions have continued to allow potentially dangerous conversions of office buildings into homes.

So far, the risk has been felt financially more than physically, with banks unwilling to provide mortgages on flats until the building has been remediated. Lucky leaseholders have found cash sellers and sold at reduced rates. The vast majority have been burdened with significant costs. Help to Buy leaseholders have found themselves trapped, with Homes England refusing to revalue their homes in the wake of the cladding scandal before conceding to pressure and allowing sales at considerably reduced rates, factoring in the costs of remediation (Simpson 2021). The taxpayer has subsidized first-time buyers and soaks up the losses. All the while, most of the blocks maintain a stay put policy. Trapped in their homes by financial straight-jackets, leaseholders have to contend with the threat of fire and a policy that defies reason. The fire safety they have comes from security guards patrolling their blocks, looking out for smoke and flames.

We might therefore be witnessing a new squalor in Britain, radiating out from the bonfire of red tape. This new squalor does not discriminate. It burns leaseholders, council tenants, housing association tenants, rent-to-buy occupants and shared owner-ships alike. The new squalor might be transcending conventional distinctions of race and class.

Remarkably, individual property owners, the very demograph-ics who have always been seen as natural Conservative voters, have been abandoned by the government in the wake of Grenfell. When one looks at the accounts of the party, it becomes clear as to why. In 2017, over a third of donations to the Conservative Party came from the corporate property sector, which is second only to the financial sector in its influence over the party.

With the Russia–Ukraine war in 2022, calls have grown to detach Russian oligarchs – lording in their London mansions – from influence over the ruling Conservative Party. Still, corpor-ate lobbying has elasticity. We should not allow sensationalism to smooth over the deeper complicities that tie government to squalor. The entire legislative structure is determined by an econ-omy utterly dependent upon speculatively increasing the value of the land beneath our feet. Grenfell remains the hard case for meaningful government reform.

When Engels (1987) coined the phrase "social murder", hous-ing was not an industry but an outcome of industrialism. Urban housing was poorly considered, planned and built, and caused preventable death. Housing might have then been ancillary to the struggle between labour and capital. However, we do not live in the nineteenth century. Capital accumulation is nowadays itself bound up with property development and land prices through financialization. In this respect, struggles over decent and afford-able housing take on a prominence once reserved only to the factory or workplace.

Cities are marked by multiple frontlines in the battle against financial capital, local government and housing organizations. Cities do not so much serve their population as mediate for capital. It is a battle that denizens are losing. Space continues to be privatized while postwar idylls are being infilled to increase housing density at the expense of any accessible public space. Towns that were made to be self-sufficient have become satellites, with 3.2 million commuters attempting to crush a daily journey of over two hours each way.

It need not be so. As the coronavirus pandemic hit, measures were taken to house the homeless, with hotels procured and buildings refashioned for the emergency. The pandemic demonstrated that with political will, such problems have solutions, even imperfect ones. We therefore call for a robust system of regulation and enforcement, which must come before the housing for the next century is built.

Is this wishful thinking?

At times, ruling elites have confronted the giant. At times, they have even induced audacious principles into the provision of housing. They have never quite managed to suspend the paternalism, racism and xenophobia that gathers around the invocation of squalor and breathes into it new life, regardless of the words uttered. Alternatively, those who struggle to enunciate an imperfect communalism – who ground themselves in their built habitat in the pursuit of justice for all – challenge us to think again about our relationship to the land, to resources, to what we value, and with whom. Confronting the dispossession of enclosure, commoners comforted themselves with a rhyme that remains suggestive of the enormity of the struggle needed to slay the giant of squalor:

> The law locks up the man or woman
> Who steals the goose off the common
> But leaves the greater villain loose
> Who steals the common from the goose.

The law demands that we atone
When we take things we do not own
But leaves the lords and ladies fine
Who takes things that are yours and mine.

The poor and wretched don't escape
If they conspire the law to break;
This must be so but they endure
Those who conspire to make the law.

The law locks up the man or woman
Who steals the goose from off the common
And geese will still a common lack
Till they go and steal it back.

References

Abel-Smith, B. 1992. "The Beveridge Report: its origins and outcomes". *International Social Security Review* 45(1/2): 5–16.

Amnesty International United Kingdom Section 2018. "Trapped in the Matrix: secrecy, stigma, and bias in the Met's gangs database". www.amnesty.org.uk/gangs.

Apps, P. 2022. "Grenfell Tower Inquiry Week 68: 'Can we agree that was a pretty dangerous thing to have, all this falling on one man's shoulders?'" *Inside Housing*. https://www.insidehousing.co.uk/insight/insight/grenfell-tower-inquiry-week-68-can-we-agree-that-was-a-pretty-dangerous-thing-to-have-all-this-falling-on-one-mans-shoulders-74764.

Bacon, R. & W. Eltis 1976. *Britain's Economic Problem: Too Few Producers*. London: Macmillan.

BBC News 2015. "Letwin apologises over 1985 Broadwater Farm riot memo". BBC News, 30 December. https://www.bbc.com/news/uk-politics-35192265.

Barker, N. 2018. "KCTMO left thousands of repairs undone, council papers reveal". *Inside Housing*, 1 December. https://www.insidehousing.co.uk/news/news/kctmo-left-thousands-of-repairs-undone-council-papers-reveal-53919.

Becker, A. 1951. "Housing in England and Wales during the Business Depression of the 1930s". *Economic History Review* 3(3): 321–41.

Begley, P. 2020. *The Making of Thatcherism: The Conservative Party in Opposition, 1974–79*. Manchester: Manchester University Press.

Bevan, N. 1946. "Nye Bevan speech." British Pathé. https://www.youtube.com/watch?v=03IlA4xoAVw.

Beveridge, W. 1942. "Social Insurances and Allied Service". DO 35/993/11. National Archives UK.

Beveridge, W. 1943. *The Pillars of Security, and Other War-Time Essays and Addresses*. London: Allen & Unwin.

Bhandar, B. 2018. "Organised state abandonment: the meaning of Grenfell". *Critical Legal Thinking*, 21 September. https://criticallegalthinking.com/2018/09/21/organised-state-abandonment-the-meaning-of-grenfell/.

Booth, C. 1897. *Life and Labour of the People in London*. London: Macmillan.

Booth, P. 2012. "The unearned increment: property and the capture of betterment value in Britain and France". In G. Ingram & Y.-H. Hong (eds), *Value Capture and Land Policies*, 74–93. Cambridge, MA: Lincoln Institute of Land Policy.

Booth, R. 2021. "Grenfell Tower landlord 'blocked staff access to residents' blog'". *The Guardian*, 27 April. https://www.theguardian.com/uk-news/2021/apr/27/grenfell-tower-landlord-blocked-staff-access-to-residents-blog.

Booth, W. 1890. *In Darkest England and the Way Out*. New York: Funk & Wagnals.

Bosanquet, B. & H. Dendy 1895. "The industrial residuum". In B. Bosanquet (ed.), *Aspects of the Social Problem*, 82–102. London: Macmillan.

Bosanquet, H. 1903. *The Strength of the People: A Study in Social Economics*. London: Macmillan.

Boughton, J. 2018. *Municipal Dreams: The Rise and Fall of Council Housing*. London: Verso.

Brown, J. 1968. "Charles Booth and labour colonies, 1889–1905". *Economic History Review* 21(2): 349–60.

Brown, L. & N. Cunningham 2016. "The inner geographies of a migrant gateway: mapping the built environment and the dynamics of Caribbean mobility in Manchester, 1951–2011". *Social Science History* 40(1): 93–120.

Bruff, I. 2014. "The rise of authoritarian neoliberalism". *Rethinking Marxism* 26(1): 113–29.

Buettner, E. 2014. "'This is Staffordshire not Alabama': racial geographies of Commonwealth immigration in early 1960s' Britain". *Journal of Imperial and Commonwealth History* 42(4): 710–40.

Carlyle, T. 1858. *Chartism: Past and Present*. London: Chapman & Hall.

Carter, B., C. Harris & S. Joshi 1987. "The 1951–55 Conservative government and the racialisation of Black immigration". Policy Papers in Ethnic Relations, University of Warwick.

Chadwick, E. 1842. *Report . . . from the Poor Law Commissioners, on an Inquiry into the Sanitary Condition of the Labouring Population of Great Britain*. London: Clowes & Sons.

Charles, M. 2016. "Grime Central! Subterranean ground-in grit engulfing manicured mainstream spaces". In K. Andrews & L. Palmer (eds), *Blackness in Britain*, 89–100. Abingdon: Routledge.

Christophers, B. 2019. *The New Enclosure: The Appropriation of Public Land in Neoliberal Britain*. New York: Verso.

Cockburn, C. 1977. "The local state: management of cities and people". *Race & Class* 18(4): 363–76.

Combe, G. 2009. *The Constitution of Man: Considered in Relation to External Objects*. Cambridge: Cambridge University Press. https://doi.org/10.1017/CBO9780511693885.

Cuming, E. 2013. "'Home is home be it never so homely': reading mid-Victorian slum interiors". *Journal of Victorian Culture* 18(3): 368–86. https://doi.org/10.1080/13555502.2013.826424.

Daffarn, E. 2020. "Second Witness Statement of Edward Daffarn". Grenfell Tower Inquiry. https://assets.grenfelltowerinquiry.org.uk/IWS00002109_Phase%202%20witness%20statement%20of%20Edward%20Daffarn.pdf.

Dickens, C. 1850. "Health by Act of Parliament". *Household Worlds* 1: 460–63.

Dorling, D. 2011. "Unique Britain". Open Democracy blog, 15 May. http://www.opendemocracy.net/ourkingdom/danny-dorling/unique-britain.

Easthope, L. 2018. *The Recovery Myth: The Plans and Situated Realities of Post-Disaster Response*. London: Palgrave Macmillan.

Ellis, D. 2017. "After Grenfell, what can we learn from the housing policies of the 1970s?" *History & Policy*, June. https://www.historyandpolicy.org/opinion-articles/articles/after-grenfell-what-can-we-learn-from-the-housing-policies-of-the-1970s.

Elmer, S. & G. Dening 2016. "The London Clearances". *City* 20(2): 271–7.

Engels, F. 1987. *The Condition of the Working Class in England*. London: Penguin.

Erlanger, S. 2015. "Release of 1985 race riots memo prompts apology from Cameron aide". *New York Times*, 30 December. https://www.nytimes.com/2015/12/31/world/europe/oliver-letwin-riots.html.

Fire Brigades Union 2019. "The Grenfell Tower fire: a crime caused by profit and deregulation." https://www.fbu.org.uk/sites/default/files/publications/The%20Grenfell%20Tower%20Fire%20A%20crime%20caused%20by%20profit%20and%20deregulation..pdf.

Garrison, L. 1979. *Black Youth, Rastafarianism, and the Identity Crisis in Britain*. London: Afro-Caribbean Education Resource Project.

Gilmore, R. 2008. "Forgotten places and the seeds of grassroots planning". In C. Hale (ed.), *Engaging Contradictions: Theory, Politics, and Methods of Activist Scholarship*, 31–61. Los Angeles, CA: University of California Press.

Ginsburg, N. 1979. *Class, Capital and Social Policy*. London: Macmillan.

Ginsburg, N. 1989. "The Housing Act, 1988 and its policy context: a critical commentary". *Critical Social Policy* 9(25): 56–81.

Glass, R. 1964. *London: Aspects of Change*. Vol. 3. London: MacGibbon & Kee.

Grindrod, J. 2014. *Concretopia: A Journey around the Rebuilding of Post-war Britian*. London: Brecon.

Hall, S. 1979. "The great moving right show". *Marxism Today*, January: 14–20.

Hall, S. *et al.* 1978. *Policing the Crisis: Mugging, The State, and Law and Order*. London: Macmillan.

Halligan, L. 2019. *Home Truths: The UK's Chronic Housing Shortage: How It Happened, Why It Matters and the Way to Solve It*. London: Biteback.

Hancock, L. & G. Mooney 2013. "'Welfare ghettos' and the 'broken society': territorial stigmatization in the contemporary UK". *Housing, Theory and Society* 30(1): 46–64.

Hanley, L. 2007. *Estates: An Intimate History*. London: Granta.

Hansard 1978. Community Land Act (Repeal), 28 February 1978. https://hansard.parliament.uk/Commons/1978-02-28/debates/8503d63a-6616-44e2-9546-431fcc97f885/CommunityLandAct(Repeal)).

Harding, J. 2020. *Post-War Homelessness Policy in the UK: Making and Implementation*. London: Palgrave Macmillan.

Harris, J. 2003. *William Beveridge: A Biography*. Oxford: Clarendon Press.

Harris, R. 2012. "'Ragged urchins play on marquetry floors': the discourse of filtering is reconstructed, 1920s–1950s". *Housing Policy Debate* 22(3): 463–82.

Harvey, D. 1982. *The Limits to Capital*. Oxford: Blackwell.

Himmelfarb, G. 1966. "The politics of democracy: the English Reform Act of 1867". *Journal of British Studies* 6(1): 97–138.

Hinton, J. 1988. "Self-help and socialism: the squatters' movement of 1946". *History Workshop Journal* 25(1): 100–126.

Historia Sanitaria 1954. "1954 – Slum Clearance". https://www.wiki.sanitarc.si/1954-slum-clearance/.

Hodkinson, S. & G. Robbins 2013. "The return of class war conservatism? Housing under the UK coalition government". *Critical Social Policy* 33(1): 57–77.

House of Lords 2016. "Building More Homes". HL Paper 20. https://publications.parliament.uk/pa/ld201617/ldselect/ldeconaf/20/2002.htm.

Inter-Departmental Committee on Physical Deterioration 1904. *Report of the Inter-Departmental Committee on Physical Deterioration*. London: Eyre & Spottiswoode.

Jacobs, B. 1984. "Labour against the centre: the Clay Cross syndrome". *Local Government Studies* 10(2): 75–87.

Jeffers, S. & P. Hoggett 1995. "Like counting deckchairs on the Titanic: a study of institutional racism and housing allocations in Haringey and Lambeth". *Housing Studies* 10(3): 325–44.

Jones, C. & A. Murie 2006. *The Right to Buy: Analysis and Evaluation of a Housing Policy*. Oxford: Blackwell.

Jones, G. 1983. *Languages of Class: Studies in English Working-Class History 1832–1982*. Cambridge: Cambridge University Press.

Joseph, K. 1974. "Speech at Edgbaston". Margaret Thatcher Foundation. https://www.margaretthatcher.org/document/101830.

Khan, S. 2017. "We owe it to the Grenfell Tower victims to establish the full truth". *The Guardian*, 18 June. https://www.theguardian.com/commentisfree/2017/jun/18/sadiq-khan-grenfell-tower-tragedy-establish-full-truth.

Koff, D. 1978. *Blacks Britannica*. London: PBS.

Kundnani, A. 2007. *The End of Tolerance: Racism in 21st Century Britain*. London: Pluto.

Lammy, D. 2017. "This was a monstrous crime – there must be arrests after Grenfell Tower". *The Guardian*, 15 June. https://www.theguardian.com/commentisfree/2017/jun/15/crime-grenfell-tower-burning-homes-police-fire.

Lefebvre, H. 1996. *Writings on Cities*. Oxford: Blackwell.

Lewis, P., M. Taylor & J. Ball 2011. "Kenneth Clarke blames English riots on a 'broken penal system'". *The Guardian*, 5 September. https://www.theguardian.com/uk/2011/sep/05/kenneth-clarke-riots-penal-system.

Mackay, R. 2003. *Half the Battle: Civilian Morale in Britain during the Second World War*. Manchester: Manchester University Press.

MacKenzie, D. 1976. "Eugenics in Britain". *Social Studies of Science* 6(3/4): 499–532.

Malik, K. 1996. *The Meaning of Race: Race, History and Culture in Western Society*. Basingstoke: Palgrave Macmillan.

Massey, D. 1980. "The pattern of landownership and its implications for policy". *Built Environment* 6(4): 263–71.

Mayhew, H. 1861. *London Labour and the London Poor*. London: Griffith, Bohn.

Mayor of London 2014. "Barriers to housing delivery – update". Greater London Authority. https://www.london.gov.uk/sites/default/files/gla_migrate_files_destination/Barriers%20to%20Housing%20Delivery%20Update%20Report%20-%20July%202014_0.pdf.

Mbembe, J. 2003. "Necropolitics". *Public Culture* 15(1): 11–40.

Morton, A. 2010. "Making housing affordable: a new vision for housing policy". London: Policy Exchange.

Newman, O. 1972. *Defensible Space: Crime Prevention through Urban Space*. New York: Macmillan.

Nicholls, G. 1899. *A History of the Poor Law: Vol III*. London: King.

O'Connell, S. 2011. "Community, race and the origins of the British credit union movement". *Quaderni Storici, Rivista Quadrimestrale* 2: 593–610.

Okri, B. 2017. "If you want to see how the poor die, come see Grenfell Tower". Public Reading Rooms. https://prruk.org/if-you-want-to-see-how-the-poor-die-come-see-grenfell-tower-by-ben-okri/.

Pepper, S. & P. Richmond 2009. "Homes unfit for heroes: the slum problem in London and Neville Chamberlain's Unhealthy Areas Committee, 1919–21". *Town Planning Review* 80(2): 143–71.

Perera, J. 2019. "The London clearances: race, housing and policing". Background Paper. London: Institute of Race Relations.

Phillipson, C. 1984. "Rethinking Beveridge: Fowler's Review of Welfare". *Critical Social Policy* 4(11): 99–102.

Pooley, S. 2013. "Parenthood, child-rearing and fertility in England, 1850–1914". *History of the Family: An International Quarterly* 18(1): 83–106.

Precey, M., J. Sturdy & L. Cawley 2019. "Inside Harlow's office block 'human warehouse' housing". BBC News. 3 April. https://www.bbc.com/news/uk-england-essex-47720887.

Prescod, C. 1985. *Struggles for Black Community*. London: Channel 4.

Reisman, D. 2001. *Richard Titmuss: Welfare and Society*. Second edition. Basingstoke: Palgrave Macmillan.

Rex, J. & R. Moore 1967. *Race, Community and Conflict: A Study of Sparkbrook*. Oxford: Oxford University Press.

Rollings, N. 1996. "Butskellism, the post-war consensus and the managed economy". In H. Jones & M. Kandiah (eds), *The Myth of Consensus*, 97–119. Basingstoke: Palgrave Macmillan.

Severs, D. 2010. "Rookeries and no-go estates: St. Giles and Broadwater Farm, or middle-class fear of 'non-street' housing". *Journal of Architecture* 15(4): 449–97.

Simpson, J. 2021. "Help to Buy leaseholders can now sell homes at 'cladding affected' value, says Homes England". Inside Housing, 10 August. https://www.insidehousing.co.uk/news/help-to-buy-leaseholders-can-now-sell-homes-at-cladding-affected-value-says-homes-england-72058.

Sivanandan, A. 1981. "From resistance to rebellion: Asian and Afro-Caribbean struggles in Britain". *Race & Class* 23(3): 111–52.

Sivanandan, A. 1990. *Communities of Resistance: Writings on Black Struggles for Socialism*. London: Verso.

Sivanandan, A. 2006. "Race, terror and civil society". *Race & Class* 47(3): 1–8.

Smith, C. 2018. *New Town Utopia*. Cult Modern.

Smith, P. 1989. "The rehousing/relocation issue in an early slum clearance scheme: Edinburgh 1865–1885". *Urban Studies* 26(1): 100–114.

Spence, L. 2016. *Knocking the Hustle: Against the Neoliberal Turn in Black Politics*. New York: Punctum.

Stein, J. 2022. "Grenfell: government official admits downplaying risk of ACM fire in UK". *Construction News* (blog), 25 March. https://www. constructionnews.co.uk/health-and-safety/grenfell-government-official-admits-downplaying-risk-of-acm-fire-in-uk-25-03-2022/.

Sunday Times 2016. "Cameron: I will bulldoze sink estates; PM's blitz on sink estates". *Sunday Times*, 10 January.

Sunstein, C. & R. Thaler 2014. *Nudge: Improving Decisions about Health, Wealth, and Happiness*. New York: Penguin.

Sutcliffe, A. & R. Walden 2021. "A vision of utopia: optimistic foundations of Le Corbusier's *Doctrine d'urbanisme*". *The Open Hand*. https://doi. org/10.1162/a8667414.add39a6f.

Taylor, J. 1986. *The Making of Modern London*. London Weekend Television.

Thomas-Symonds, N. 2015. *Nye: The Political Life of Aneurin Bevan*. London: I. B. Tauris.

Timmins, N. 2001. *The Five Giants: A Biography of the Welfare State*. London: HarperCollins.

Topalov, C. 1993. "The city as terra incognita: Charles Booth's poverty survey and the people of London, 1886–1891". *Planning Perspectives* 8(4): 395–425.

Tunstall, R. 2015. "The coalition's record on housing: policy, spending and outcomes 2010–2015". Working Paper 18. Centre for Housing Policy.

Unwin, R. 2014. *Nothing Gained by Overcrowding*. Abingdon: Routledge.

White, R. 2018. "Another step towards land market reform". Shelter (blog), 13 September. https://blog.shelter.org.uk/2018/09/another-step-towards-land-market-reform/.

Wohl, A. 1971. "Octavia Hill and the homes of the London poor". *Journal of British Studies* 10(2): 105–31.

Wolfinden, R. 1946. "Problem families". *Eugenics Review* 38(3): 127–32.

Women's Group on Public Welfare 1943. *Our Towns: A Close-Up*. Oxford: Oxford University Press.

Wood, E. 1934. "A century of the housing problem". *Law and Contemporary Problems* 1(2): 137–47.

Wrack, M. 2018. "Deregulation and the Grenfell Tower fire". Fire Brigades Union (blog), 20 June. https://www.fbu.org.uk/blog/deregulation-and-grenfell-tower-fire.

Index